*for darling A
and all my
a eve
fine*

SOFIA: PORTRAIT OF A CITY

Of all major European capitals, Sofia has always remained the least known, the least familiar. The capital of Bulgaria since 1879, it numbers over a million, or more than one in nine of the country's population.

Settlements have existed here, below Mount Vitosha, for eight thousand years, but it is only within the last century that Sofia (borrowing its name from the Greek word for wisdom, and the original Byzantine church at its heart) has grown to its present eminence among Bulgarian cities, on the highway from Belgrade in the north to Athens in the south.

A constant procession of civilisations has left marks throughout Sofia, from the Serdi to the Greeks and Romans, the Slavs, Byzantines, Bulgarians immigrating from the East, and the Ottomans over 500 years.

Philip Ward, author of the award-winning *Bulgaria: A Travel Guide*, has revisited Sofia many times in the course of writing his books, including *Bulgarian Voices*, and here evokes the atmosphere of museums and churches, architectural enclaves and parks, streets and cafés, looking, learning, and listening. He talks to a democratic activist, a champion angler, a watermelon-seller, an army colonel, and operatic madman. He enjoys the village of Simeonovo, the health resort of Bankya, and wayside bookstalls.

Anyone trying to understand the city and people of Sofia would benefit from the wry, appreciative but occasionally sardonic view of a travel writer whose books on Japan, India, Libya, Oman, Saudi Arabia, Finland and Sicily's Aeolian Islands have made him popular among independent travellers the world over. His previous 'portraits of a city' covered *Tripoli* and *Bangkok*.

PHILIP WARD, FRSA, FRGS, ALA, is a well-known authority on Eastern Europe, having written the first modern guide to *Albania* (1983), *Polish Cities* (1988), and *Bulgaria* (1989). His *Bulgarian Voices* (1992), set mainly in Sofia, is an edited compendium of Bulgarians' lives and opinions in their own words. He has lived abroad for many years, mainly in Asia and Africa, and has visited the U.S.S.R., Hungary and Czechoslovakia. He is a long-term member of the British-Bulgarian Friendship Society and the Bulgarian-British Club in Plovdiv.

SOPHIA.

УЛИЦА ТЪРГОВСКА.
Handelsstrasse.

SOFIA
Portrait of a City

Philip Ward

***

THE OLEANDER PRESS LTD

The Oleander Press
17 Stansgate Avenue
Cambridge CB2 2QZ
England

The Oleander Press
80 Eighth Avenue (Suite 303)
New York, N.Y. 10011
U.S.A

British Library Cataloguing in Publication Data

Ward, Philip
   Sofia: Portrait of a City. – (Oleander Travel Books Series; v.20)
   I. Title II. Series
   914.9773

   ISBN 0-906672-65-1

Typeset, printed and bound in Great Britain

CONTENTS

ACKNOWLEDGMENTS AND INTRODUCTION

My thanks are as always warmly directed towards friends and colleagues of the State Company Touristreklama; to my landlady D.S. who made my long stay so agreeable; to Belin Mollov who spoke of the long-term plans for Sofia as we gazed out from his window down to the Church of the Holy Wisdom that gave this city its name; to Margarita Koeva for visits in her well-informed and vivacious company to the architectural complexes around Ulitsa Oborishte and Ulitsa 3 April, to Yordanka Kotseva for first initiating me into the most recondite corners of Sofia many years ago, and to all those who gave me planned or spontaneous hospitality from Lyulin to Mladost. Some names have been changed to avoid possible embarrassment and some names have been omitted altogether at their request.

Iliana Atanassova gave me unexpected help when it was most needed with interpreting, contacts, co-ordination and endless hard work behind the scenes, few of which failed to materialise even though many Bulgarians have to take a second job to make ends meet. For use of her valuable time, and theirs, no thanks could be too munificent.

Mariana Marinova, Curator of Collections, Museum of the City of Sofia, kindly accompanied me to the prehistoric site of Slatina.

I thank Elinka Boyajieva, Director of the Museum of the City of Sofia, 'Grigor' and the Colonel, Dr Krassen Stanchev of Ecoglasnost, Georgi Bozhinov, Milcho Katsov, Rossitsa Zlatanova, Pepi Ivanova and her mother, 'Vera' of the Centre for Bulgarian Studies, Delyana Simeonova and Daniela Nedyalkova. Lidia Ivanova gave me a great deal of help, and as always I relied on the courtesy and dependability of Valentina Kanazirska.

This is my third book about Bulgaria, which must seem odd to those who know me as a specialist on Indian travel, private libraries, Spanish literature, common fallacies, and the Arabian Peninsula. The reason is that, in the course of traversing the length and breadth of the country for *Bulgaria: a Travel Guide* (Oleander of Cambridge, 1989: Pelican, U.S.A. 1990) and *Bulgarian Voices* (Oleander of Cambridge, 1992), I came to love Sofia inordinately, irrationally, more perhaps because of the people, like Dragan Tenev and Ana Bogdanova, Slavimir Genchev and Borianna Hristova, than for any monuments or architectural style.

'Life is somewhat undramatic,' noted Brecht. 'It does not know Yes or No, White or Black, All or Nothing.' Much of Sofia, thankfully, confirms Brecht's dictum. If you avoid gazing up at Vitosha's white virgin wilderness in January, or gazing down at an alcoholic stubbly on a park bench, mutely appealing for miracles. The frequent clanking of trams are undramatic, like the shelves of department stores. But daily lives seem dramatic enough, as you hear of whole families emigrating to Australia, or starting new private businesses in computers or tourism.

Sofia's name is aptly borrowed from the Greek for wisdom: it often strikes me that the notion rubs off on many citizens, whose levelheadedness made it possible for the unfamiliar phenomenon of parliamentary elections to occur in an atmosphere of calm. Sofiotes behave peacefully, tolerantly, gently, stably and farsightedly, by and large. I attended demonstrations for the Union of Democratic Forces and the Bulgarian Socialist Party on consecutive evenings in Battenberg Square, and found the atmosphere of each celebratory and festive, communicating jovial solidarity. Their rivals stayed away, avoiding violence or even confrontation. Such reasonable conviviality has characterised most Bulgarians throughout the ages.

LIST OF ILLUSTRATIONS

1: VERA FINDS AN APARTMENT

My friend Vera met me at the Airport. 'I was hoping you'd be on this plane, because you weren't on the morning flight from London.'

'There *is* no morning flight from London. We come back from Heathrow on the same plane that leaves Sofia in the morning.'

'Yes, but I didn't know that. Come with me and we'll find the bus to the centre. From Eagles' Bridge we can walk to your apartment. I've found you a comfortable place on Bulevard Knyaz Dondukov'.

'That's marvellous: just close to the Opera on the corner of Rakovski.'

'I haven't been inside, but the woman at Balkantourist with private accommodation said that it costs six dollars a night, so it must be de luxe.'

'What about the bus fare?'

'Have you got any bus tickets?'

'No, I've just arrived from London.'

'You can't pay with money, you have to show tickets.'

'Can the driver sell us two tickets?'

'No, he doesn't carry any cash, especially at night.'

'What about in the daytime?'

'Especially in the daytime, with all those passengers.'

Vera now engaged in earnest conversation with the driver, who was sitting on the kerb, chainsmoking.

'He says we can only get on the bus if we have tickets. But it's all right, because you're a foreigner and you don't know anything.' I heaved my suitcase up into the dark, empty bus and waited for the inertia to stop.

I ruminated on my apartment's key, which had a label reading 'Krumova, Bul Dondukov, 89 entrance B.'

Bulevard Dondukov (corner of Volgograd)

Vera pursed her lips. 'That telephone number doesn't work', she warned me. The label, as I held it, detached itself from the key.

'Do you know the Krumovi family?'

'No, I think they're from Kyustendil, the grandmother Mariana I think she doesn't live longer, the mother Rosinka I think she's there by her own, and the daughter Elena I think she has too many problems with her family.'

'What else don't you remember about them?'

'Well, for sure they must be connected with Balkantourist, because too many people would want to let out their rooms for six dollars if they had the good chance.'

The driver screwed his diminutive fagend below his nostalgic foot, sighed, and got on to his bus as though a stranger there himself.

From several dark corners of the airport small rodentlike people poured on to the bus as the driver engaged gear, filling every seat and gangway with themselves and rustling

Orlov Most (Eagles' Bridge)

parcels wrapped in brown paper, and sharp-edged boxes of what looked to be nitroglycerine.

We turned the corner and bowled along the wide boulevard towards the city centre, between mile after mile of anonymous winking-windowed multi-storey apartments blocks robbed of their shabbiness by the early evening's soft, velvety purple.

'It's good to be back in Sofia, Vera.'

'I last saw you on 4 June, that's three months ago.'

'Why did Professor Petrov say that all my plans had been cancelled?'

'There's no more money for visiting scholars, so we've had

to cancel everyone from all over the world for the rest of the year.'

'So what will the Centre for Bulgarian Studies do, without any money, close down?'

'I don't know, Professor Petrov is still on holiday and he won't be back for a long time.'

'What about Professor Mihailov who promised to help with meetings when I saw him in June?'

'He's been sacked, I don't know why, but it may be something to do with the Communists.'

'Which is which, Mihailov or Petrov?'

'I don't know, but I have a lot of contacts and I always think if you want to meet actors and writers and opera-singers, it's better not to arrange things beforehand, but to take them by surprise, like that *Alice in Wonderland* book you gave me.'

'We can get out here, Vera, this is Eagles' Bridge.'

'It's not too far to walk. But I don't think Krumova is at home. I hope she hasn't bolted the place up like a fortress, so you can't get in.'

'Like that *Count of Monte Cristo* I gave you', I interrupted, and she giggled.

2: A FRIENDLY LIFT

Among my friends, I enjoy a notoriety for clumsiness bord-
ering on the legendary, and an ineptitude with mechanical
objects that would make the sorcerer's apprentice of Dukas
look like a computer wizard. Did I say mechanical? I only
learned how to tie my own shoelaces at the age of eleven
when confronted by the need to wear football boots on the
school playing-field.

So it was no surprise to me that I could not make the lift
up to the fourth floor at Bulevard Dondukov 89, entrance B,
utter more than a faint, disgusted whir before petering out
into total silence. 'Stille Nacht, Heilige Nacht', I hummed.

Vera observed, 'This lift it does not work yet.'

I tried pushing all the other buttons, as well as number 4.
Nothing happened. Vera tried the same, muttering accus-
ingly about licences from foreign companies to make their
lifts in Sofia which were not worth the paper they were written on. 'All these lifts used to work one day,' she grumbled,
'Otherwise how do people get upwards?'

'Possibly by the stairs,' I hazarded, apologetically. After all,
Vera had a husband and child to go home to, and here I was,
imprisoning her in a claustrophobic limbo. For anyone who
chose to gaze through the porthole into the murky lift, our
necessary proximity must have seemed compromising. I
momentarily forgot in my panic the Bulgarian for 'we're just
good friends'.

And then the lift lurched and began to rise, vibrating like
the massage belt in a Stan Laurel movie. One of us must
have pressed a significant button. 'I think it's the second
floor'. I forced open the wooden slatted door, and pushed open
the main door, inching my way forward to investigate the
names on the doors for a clues. A shaft of light illuminated

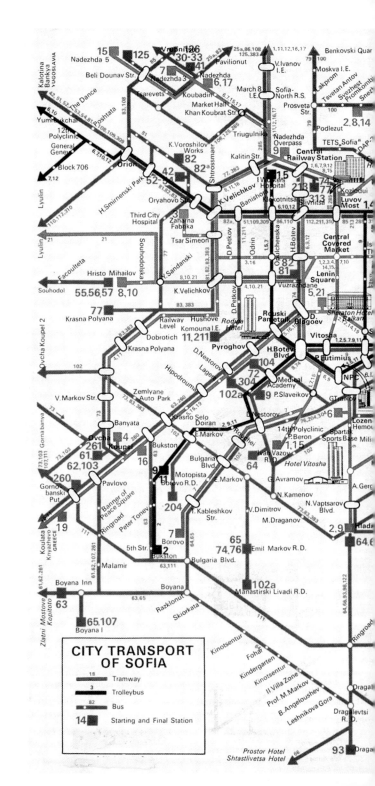

CITY TRANSPORT
OF SOFIA

	Tramway
	Trolleybus
	Bus
14	Starting and Final Station

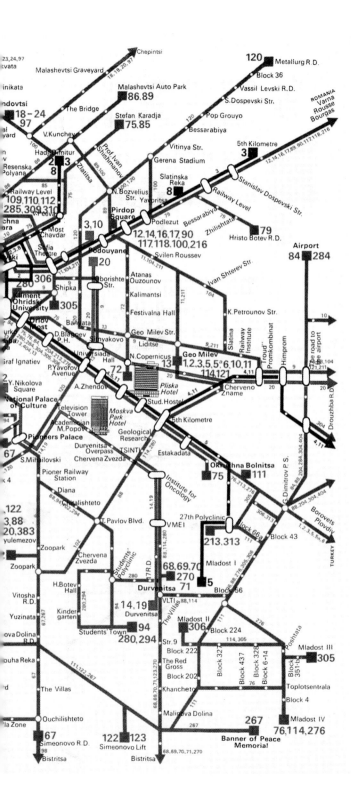

the number '3' by the stairwell. I bounded back in.

'Just one more', I said cheerfully, knocking my chin on my suitcase and clanging the wooden door shut.

I felt for the button below the top one, which destined the daring for the fifth storey. I pushed it, and lo! The lift moved. 'We're here!' I cried, in a carefree manner that my friends have grown to mistrust. We were, indeed, in a manner of speaking there. We were so firmly and completely there that, although I could wiggle the slatted door robustly both to and fro, the outer door wouldn't budge a millimetre.

'Um, zdravei!' I muttered uncertainly at non-existent passers-by. 'Dobur vecher!'

Vera said, 'Do you think we should scream?'

'Definitely not,' I answered. 'Anyone with an ounce of imagination would instantly guess what you were screaming about, and I'd be on the next plane back to Heathrow. I suggest a kind of polite coughing, just enough to attract forgiving attention.'

Some fourteen minutes later by my luminous watch a door opened. Friend or foe? It turned out to be friend Damyan Volkov from number 37.

'Ne trudno,' he roared at us in our dark lift. 'You just press the little spring at the top right while touching the alarm button and the door springs open.'

I followed regulations and the lift swiftly and efficiently returned to the ground floor where the Ribarovi from 43 and the Elenkovi from 44 had patiently been awaiting developments.

'Here', said a large dark body. 'You push button for the fifth floor, and then walk down the stairs till you come to the fourth.'

After two or three weeks of this, my cackhandedness and the unfailing if varied advice from the Boichevi, the Georgievi, the Maslenkovi, the Ivanovi, the Nikolovi, the Shotovi and the Alexandrovi had made me so many firm friends that, once they had recovered from their fits of laughter, they would invite me in for rakia, vodka, and Coca Cola, or, if they were on their way out, treat me, protest though I might, to a healing brew of black coffee at the Café Edelweiss on the corner of Dondukov and Biryuzov. It is still the friendliest lift I know.

3: SLEEPING BETWEEN THE TRAMS

One of the arts of finding yourself private accommodation in Sofia is craftily to enquire whether it's handy for the trams. If so, my advice is to steer well clear. Even on the fourth floor, sparks from the night trams on Bulevard Dondukov lit up the night sky like Guy Fawkes' bonfires, and made slumber virtually impossible up to about one a.m., when the regular trams come to a stop, and after approximately four, when the regular trams start up again. You really have to sleep between the trams.

Since 'the events of 1989', as the fall of Todor Zhivkov is universally described, there has been a further brainwave for tramfanciers. Women out late at night, because of shiftwork or other necessities, have been campaigning for years for a night relief tram at less frequent intervals, so even the depths of night are scarred and pitted by the noisy racket of trams as they screech and brake along the cobbled centres of main thoroughfares. Like Bulevard Dondukov. You now have to catch a few winks between trams, forty being somewhat ambitious.

The yellow trams so familiar to travellers have been painted red now, advertising a brand of American cigarettes.

So I slept fitfully, the moon peering in through curtains I could never quite close, on a hard bed transformed into a sofa during the day. There were two single beds: one below the wide window and one at right angles. Opposite, the 'red' newspaper *Trud* ('Labour') ground out its steadily decreasing print-run, its stalwart Communism under steadily increasing pressure from the horde of new democratic newspapers appealing to all sectors of the 'blue' or democratic market. In the morning, on my way to pick up a fresh loaf, some fruit, and a delicious yoghurt, I would pass the vendor of *Trud* out-

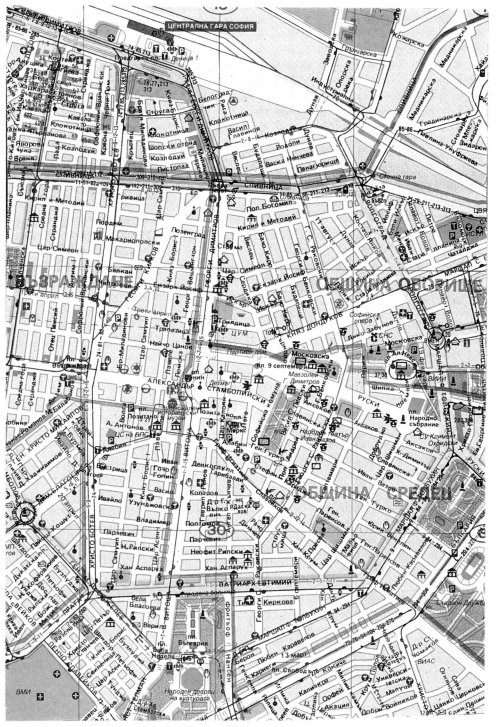

Map of Sofia City Centre

Tram number 10

side the front door, half a dozen copies still moist from the press, an enamel mug still empty of coins beside the yawning salesman, his tight-fitting jacket and ill-fitting trousers symbolising the fact that *Trud* no longer seems to fit the time.

I brewed tea on the electric hotplate, mixed honey with my yoghurt in the Greek manner, spread fig jam on my white bread, and failed to get a murmur from the telephone. It was permanently dead. My landlady Rosinka was not expected back yet, explained the woman behind the counter at Balkantourist, farther along Dondukov, and I couldn't phone from there because only official business could be transacted by official phones.

I paid US$6 a night for three weeks' accommodation, exchanged travellers' cheques for leva at the counter nearby, the official rate being about 30 leva to the £1, or 18 to the US$1, and ran along Dondukov to my friends at the Touristreklama State Company, Georgi Stoyanov, Valya Kanazirska, Moni Dimitrov.

'All my plans for writing a book on Sofia seem to have been torpedoed by the Centre for Bulgarian Studies,' I explained, 'and I wonder what we can do to rescue it?'

'Here is Lidia Ivanova', said Moni. 'You tell us what you want, and we'll try to organise it from here, and Lidia will help you day by day.'

'I'd like to start before history,' I said. 'Before Sofia was so called in the 14th century, before Slavonic Sredets, before Roman Serdica, when Neolithic people settled in the zone nowadays called Slatina.'

4: THE DISCOVERY OF SLATINA

You take the number 20 tram to the stop called Geo Milev, then walk away from the city past the Institute for Mechanics and Biomechanics, keeping on the right-hand side of the highway, then climbing a slope until you come to a collection of huts, protected by wire fencing. This is Slatina, 8,000 years ago a large Early Neolithic village, which survived the Middle Neolithic and spread during the Late Neolithic towards the south, covering an area of at least eighty thousand square metres.

Slatina, now within the territory of the City of Sofia, was situated in a fertile plain watered by rivers and mineral springs at the foot of Mount Vitosha. 'Slatina' indeed denotes a spring, or source. At that time forests would have extended down here, with abundant game, yet the modern city centre was also evidently populated: archaeologists working in 9 September Square have turned up Early Neolithic sherds. Slatina's earliest finds include female cult figurines of the type associated by some scholars with the idea of a mother goddess.

Slatina was discovered in the late 1920s during railway diggings, first excavated in 1932 by the amateur Nedelcho Petkov, neglected until 1959, reopened by Petkov again in that year, and first professionally explored by Vassil Nikolov in 1985, when new digging for a tramline made rescue operations urgent. Excavations under the auspices of the Museum of the City of Sofia have taken place for three months every year since then, and huge quantities of finds are stored and classified in temporary rooms not yet open to the unaccompanied public.

The major discovery is an Early Neolithic dwelling area measuring 1500 square metres on the northwest periphery of

Slatina. Female terracotta figurines

the site, that is on the west bank of the river. It consists of five cultural levels and work proceeds now on the highest, or latest, level. At the second level, Professor Nikolov has identified a cult object connectable with a temple: a podium bears a column with a triangular relief, unique for this period, around 6,000 B.C. in Bulgaria and the Middle East. Each of the nine surrounding houses has a clay vessel or animal bones buried under the west or northwest corner, suggesting to Nikolov a sacrificial victim. Then the Slatinites built a clay floor on which wooden and wattle-and-daub structures were raised for dwellings, for grain storehouses, and possibly for domesticated animals, indicated by little zoomorphic terracottas of goats, sheep and bulls. Bone beads from necklaces, obsidian imported from the Aegean or Mediterranean, sherds from a pot which may have represented a buffalo, brown and red painted vessels with lighter colours of the earlier phase and darker from the later phase: these are significant finds shown me by Krum Bachvarov and Emilia Sirakova.

The houses are oriented north-west: the wind direction in this valley. The one-roomed houses have an entrance on the south. Of the three most interesting burials, that of a woman about 40 was annihilated when they made the rail track. A young man of 20 was buried with flint knives and a double-faced stamp in terracotta without parallel. A young woman of 18 or so was buried in a manner totally unlike others, face down and contracted, head facing east and legs west.

The two-room house uncovered in 1985 contained a stone axe, part of a plough, knives of bone, flint and horn, tools for making flint implements, and weights for vertical looms. Cult objects in the south-east corner included a steatopygous goddess and a terracotta bull. A large sherd, possibly from a grain-jar, bore the impress of two hands with four woman's fingers and three man's fingers possibly to appease the spirit-guardian of the house. A similar fertility cult was identified by the late Professor Georgi Georgiev at the site of Kremikovtsi in 1958.

So far Slatina has yielded more than two thousand objects, such as very fine spatulae, tools for pottery-making, and a rich variety of arrowheads. Apart from obsidian, there are no definite indications of imported goods, but there are satisfying parallels with the rich material culture of other sites in north-west Bulgaria such as Gradeshnitsa.

Seventy workers used to be employed on the site at 12 leva daily (enough to buy two loaves), but with increased financial stringency their numbers are down to eight, and Mrs Kounka Grigorova, who retired some months ago as the archaeologist representing the Museum of the City of Sofia, has come back to lend her considerable experience.

After showing me around, the archaeologists treated me to coffee and biscuits in their shady bower fragrant with red roses, and spoke of the similar Neolithic site of Tell Karanovo, in the area of Nova Zagora, which has been excavated annually since 1984 by a joint Austrian-Bulgarian team.

5: COFFEE WITH AN ACTIVIST

Every time I visit Sofia I am baffled by attitudes to time. On one hand, if you have to moonlight to make ends meet, every second must be worth money. If you have to travel two hours to work, using three trams across the city, those hours are virtually worthless. If you have to stand in a queue for two hours, your send in your granny. Employees often do a second job while at work, if the boss turns a blind eye in exchange for your never asking him why he takes a four-hour lunch or leaves two hours early. If you have family problems, health problems, emotional problems, discreet allowances are made. Time and again I found younger brothers and sisters studying in the evenings and working by day because the family's money for education had all been spent on the eldest child. A single mother with a child is allowed official time off, then unofficial time. Someone in the office is allowed to go shopping, if others in the office can share the result. Friends and families give food, give parties, in an endless whirl of unspoken bartering.

When I visit, I take expensive coffee in exchange for the time my hostess has spent preparing for me an extra place at the family table. Lunches will often be short, unless service is incompetent, because diners are off somewhere else. Dinners will usually be long, because they are social occasions for bonding, reciprocating hospitality and renewing friendships.

Some Bulgarians have absolutely no idea of punctuality. Others make a real effort to be punctual. If you have to meet someone you don't know, you have the choice of coming too late, or hanging around looking at your watch. My method in Sofia is to arrive on time and bring plenty of writing-paper and a good book, or speak with someone nearby who looks interesting, beautiful, or both. There is no shortage of such

17

happy informal contacts. Indeed, most of my best Bulgarian friends are acquaintances.

Yet Bulgarians are impulsively generous with their time: none more touchingly so than Milcho Katsov, who agreed to give me two hours of his time while dramatically busy with his (successful) campaign to promote the election of the Philip Dimitrov branch of the Union of Democratic Forces.

Born in Sofia in 1955, with a neat clothes-hanger-shaped moustache and a dapper suit, he graduated in the geography of tourism at Sofia University in 1979, and has been working at Pirintourist ever since. Unmarried, he had dedicated his previous two years to the Havel-like civic committees, which he had helped found in February 1990. These committees run parallel with the political Union and include everyone desirous of fighting Communism. Of the 1700 voters in Milcho's Ruski Pametnik (Russian Monument) constituency, 400 have already signed up as active members of the civic committee, which is impressive when one recalls that the idea only originated a few months back.

Milcho described his enthusiasm for Vaclav Havel's populist approach. 'A civic committee can include anyone, even if he is not a member of a pro-democratic party. I for example was a member of Milan Drenchev's party but in this election I do not support him because I am against the party principle. It is too early in our democratic process to have parties. Of Bulgaria's population, we have a 3% educated élite; the other 97% are newly liberated serfs. We had a feudal peasantry under Communism because they were hired labour who didn't own the land they worked. Now with land reform, we shall give them land if they never had any, or give back land if they were former landowners.'

'The main aim of civic committees is to prevent the politicization of life in the country. People should get on with their job, not work for mastodon parties. Civic committees are intended to unite members of differing political factions against the common enemy of totalitarianism.'

'I believe the Communist Party should not be abolished be-

Milcho Katsov

cause it is a semi-military organisation founded at the end of
the 19th century for the purpose of underground struggle and
its only aim to is get and retain power. Its means of struggle

19

are three: confrontation, agent provocation and discredita-tion. If you ban such an organisation it will inevitably return underground which is its natural habitat, it will thrive there, and revive to subvert again during the following generation. Our Bulgarian tragedy is that after the Communists des-troyed their democratic opponents in the 1940s, we had abso-lutely no durable, widespread underground opposition, and that is why the Opposition did not win more than a narrow victory at the recent elections in October 1991. The Commun-ists, though not too popular, proved to be much better or-ganised with their long experience.'

'Bulgarian communists are cleverer than Russians; for one thing, our Party has a much longer tradition, and organised its Agrarian opponents into a rubber-stamping party which issued token challenges but on any major issue could always be relied on to vote with the Communists. That was the con-dition by which they were allowed to survive and prosper.'

'The Communists are not worried about trying to dominate Bulgarian radio and TV because the media are controlled by the Karakachanov and Dertliev wings of the Union of Demo-cratic Forces and those wings already discredit the Union by their pro-leftist sympathies. Interestingly, Communist tactics to delay and postpone change in the period 1989-91 have not worked, so it will be interesting to see what they try next.'

'As for our minorities, we now have to face up to the exist-ence of Turks, Armenians, Jews and gipsies, and to allow them their own culture, languages, and their own unity to promote their self-interest, just as we Bulgarians do. Because the Turks will never have more than 10% of the vote, they will do well to align themselves permanently with the U.D.F. In the past, the Turkish lobby within other parties has helped pro-Turkish legislation, and I am not sure that having a much more vocal and visible presence will benefit them: it may provoke an anti-Turkish backlash in the majority.'

'The monarchy is not yet a live issue, because its suppor-ters still total less than 20%. I don't mind whether we have a parliamentary monarchy or a parliamentary republic. We have suffered under both monarchist and republican dictators so the issue is not so much about the figurehead of state, but the strength and continuity of the parliamentary system, with a viable government in office and responsible opposition. Actually, I'm not keen on any kind of figurehead, but it seems that Bulgarians yearn for a strong hand above them. We like bowing to someone. We always ask, "Who's the boss?"'

'What is the Bulgarian national character? We used to work very hard, but under Communism this tendency has vanished, and now a few people work hard for others, many more work hard only for themselves, but the majority have lost the habit of hard work altogether. On the positive side, our hospitality has never diminished over the years. We always know how to treat foreigners well, and other Bulgarians too.'

'Don't you find Sofia extraordinarily patriarchal, Milcho? When the rest of Europe is trying to break down chauvinist attitudes, they seem to be hardening here.'

'I don't believe there is any clear tendency towards patriarchy or matriarchy. Communism was sexless: it built not on sex difference or sex exploitation, but on fear. Women, told they would be the equals of men, ended up being turned into slaves – just like the men were. A woman was told that her work was equally valuable, deserved equal pay (as long as her quotas weren't down), but what they didn't explain was that *in addition* to all this splendid equality of opportunity at work, she would have to drudge in the home just as much as ever before. She became a de facto slave twice over. *Before Communism*, I'd agree that Bulgaria was patriarchal, but our chaotic society is now so fluid that no clear tendency emerges. Once we had a normal Bulgarian extended family of a man, woman, two children and one or two parents. *That doesn't exist any more.* The oldest man used to be head of the family, but in a rather symbolic sense. The oldest son would stay with the family and the younger men would go away. Until World War II the three-generation structure lingered in both town and country; now that type is disappearing everywhere.'

'There is a widespread theory that Bulgarians have an innate love for jokes, and it is precisely by this mechanism of turning disaster and despair into comedy that we have remained sane. It has worked ideally so far and it will remain a necessity, not a virtue.'

'Milcho, how do you compare Sofia with other capitals?'

'In 1987 I was suspected as a potential trouble-maker, and prevented from crossing to Western Europe, although as a tour operator it was actually my job. I needed to go to Vienna, but they refused to give me a visa. Instead, on a caprice, the authorities sent me with a group to Pyongyang, capital of North Korea, at the other end of the world, an opportunity I should never have had otherwise.'

'Militant communism and the personality cult were so manic that not only did I find a portrait of Kim Il Sung in every room, but the frame is so tilted in your bedroom that even when you are lying down the face seems to be watching you.'

'In Pyongyang everyone is assured of the basics of life, but the catch is that children are removed from their families at the age of five months and sent back only at eighteen when fully trained in the theory and practice of devotion to the Great Leader and the Dear Leader. The state watches over every aspect of bringing up: schooling (one cannot of course call it education in any broad sense), food and clothing. At the age of four they attend kindergarten classes with a special room for studying the works of Kim Il Sung. What attracts me to the Juche Idea of Kim Il Sung is the belief that if people are free from everyday worries they become creative. That's why all housing is state-owned and why rice costs next to nothing. As we queue for everyday necessities and find their prices rise almost daily and the poorest become even poorer, such notions become dangerously attractive.'

Milcho and I sat on a podium; dark spread from the corners of the hall on Ulitsa Sandor Petöfi into the centre, and individuals drifted in from the street for the evening meeting of their local civic committee.

We discussed economics, politics, tourism and society, literature and art, music and psychology: it was the kind of conversation that lifts the spirit with its swift changes of mood, its rainbows of humour and storms of solemn worry. He had been as candid with me as any man could be; he seemed to unstained by cynicism yet clear-seeing, without the illusions of party bias that simpler souls carry with them to the grave in the belief that such prejudices do them some obscure kind of credit. Working together no matter what: that was Milcho's message.

6: THRACIAN AND ROMAN SERDICA

We cannot be certain whether multiple migration gave us the south-eastern Europe population we know today, or whether indigenous populations developed with relatively minor incursions from outside. The first theory is attractive to those who observe gaps in occupation settlements, which could of course be due to natural disasters or innate human wanderlust; the second appeals to those noting continuities at other sites. If we accept both in the absence of incontrovertible evidence, we arrive at the suggestion that settled populations were constantly joined by immigrants who strengthened local communities by intermarriage and new technologies.

Though westerners are familiar with the civilizations of the Greeks and Romans, we tend to neglect the Thracians, whose tribes colonised most of present-day Bulgaria at least as early as the 8th century B.C. according to Homer and almost certainly even earlier than that.

Modern Bulgarian territory was their heartland but evidence for their first dispersal can be found throughout the Eastern Mediterranean, Caucasus and south-eastern Europe in the form of linguistic, mythographic and archeological data. A second great dispersal of the Thracians coincides with Alexander the Great's expeditions in the East, and the early Roman Empire, as proved by papyri, coins, inscriptions and archaeological data. Their religious system and social customs were by now clearly defined, and are analysed thoroughly in *Thrace and the Thracians* by Alexander Fol and Ivan Marazov (London, 1977). A third dispersal occurred during the separation of the Eastern Roman Empire from the Western, and is recorded by texts from late antiquity.

The second book of the *Iliad* delineates Thrace within a small area, but by the late sixth century B.C. the name had come to designate all the territory south of the Danube (Istros in Greek) and its inhabitants. Homer names only three tribes: Thracians, Cicones and Paeones, but Herodotus lists twelve and the later Hellenistic geographers counted eighty, as centralised structures broke up and local clans or tribes claimed local hegemony.

The National History Museum in Sofia is crammed with Thracian art treasures, and copies from treasures held in regional museums. Northern Bulgarian Thracian tribes were called Triballi, Moesi and Getae. In Southern Bulgaria, again roughly west-east, the main tribes were the Serdi around present-day Sofia, the Bessi and Odrysi. Thus did the Romans know the place as 'the town of the Serdi' or Serdica. Thracian culture is known to have reached its zenith under the fifth-century Odrysi, who created a material civilisation hardly less interesting or worth study than that of their contemporaries in Greece, who minted coins at roughly the same moment.

At this distance we can only speculate on Thracian religion, for written records are few and patchy. But there is no doubt that they worshipped a God-Hero-Horseman, and revered a Mother Goddess who may be associated with a lover-son in a mode we in our Hellenocentric way connect with Jocasta and Oedipus. Dionysus is as much Thracian as Greek, but he came from Asia Minor, if not from farther east.

Thracian Serdica has been lost, below the surface of present-day Sofia, except for that faint reluctant corner of the Roman city, like the corner of a page turned over to mark a place, between the triangular tower under the Sofia Shop and the Roman Western Gate near the junction of Ulitsa Lavele and Ulitsa 3 April. The Serdi resisted mightily, but in the first century A.D. the Romans exerted their military might and chose Serdica as their district capital. The Thracian language persisted in the countryside, much as Celtic languages survived the Roman invasion in Britain, but the learned, administrative and military language became Latin. Trajan (98-117) gave his epithet Ulpius as an honorific to Serdica

Ulpia and the city – like contemporary Philippopolis to the east – acquired theatres, amphitheatres, basilicas, baths, temples, wide streets and squares, villas and forums. In the 2nd century A.D., during the joint reign of Marcus Aurelius and Commodus, a higher, thicker wall went up to protect Serdica from raiding invaders. This, with its great eastern and western gateways, can still be seen in vestigial form today: you can superimpose on your modern plan of the city, an approximate rectangle (with that missing northwest Thracian scrag-end) with its northern boundary along Exarch Yosif Street, east from the round tower on Exarch Yosif down to just north of Alabin, then a southern boundary crossing Bulevard Vitosha, and its western side touching the eastern side of Ulitsa Lavele till you reach the western gateway. The most spectacular Roman complex in the city is that behind the Sheraton Hotel, permanently open to the public.

Part of the eastern gateway can be seen in the carefully-preserved underground passages near the former headquarters of the Bulgarian Communist Party where Dondukov meets Ruski. The wall is dated 176-180 by a Greek inscription displayed in this underpass:

Good fortune. The most great, the divine Emperor Caesar Marcus Aurelius Antoninus Augustus, conqueror of the Sarmatians, the Germans, Father of the Fatherland and High Priest, and Emperor Aurelius Commodus Augustus, conqueror of the Sarmatians and the Germans, endowed the town of the Serdi with city walls during the governorate of Aurelianus Aemilianus.

This first wall consisted of massive stone blocks and a brick superstructure two metres thick. It was replaced around the year 300 by a new wall about 11 metres high and 2½ metres thick, alternating stone and brick: a serious obstacle to invaders seeking to breach the peace of Roman Serdica, with sixteen round towers at least; there may have been more. Siege methods apparently improved, because the defenders added a further thickness of 1.8 metres of durable brick around the year 500, and a new series of triangular towers, plus a few pentagonal towers.

But the massive eastern gateway you see protected below ground dates from Justinian's time (527-565), when the balance of power had shifted from Rome to Constantinople. You can still see grooves where the portcullis was raised and dropped. If you wander now to the western gateway, you will find its ruins at the confluence of Ulitsa Knyaz Boris I, Trapezitsa and George Washington. Large blocks of limestone formed this massive gateway, which was strengthened on many occasions between the second century and the 14th. It suffered its last undermining and capture in 1382, when the Ottomans concluded a successful three-month siege.

If you feel like walking along the main thoroughfare of Roman Serdica, just visit the basement of Bulevard Vitosha 1. The old paving stones remain in place above a well-planned sewer system connected with an underground shaft at the end of the street, and a bricklined water-supply system with terracotta piping in double and triple rows from a catchment in the Vitosha foothills. Constantine the Great (306-337) declared: 'Serdica is my Rome' and his Serdica was splendidly endowed with baths, though nothing like the grandiose complex at Varna has been uncovered. Some thermae chambers and a hypocaust of the 4th century were discovered below Sofia's Hali, or Covered Market, near the Banya Bashi Mosque.

Of the same date are the churches of Hagia Sophia, or the Holy Wisdom, set in an early Christian necropolis; and St George, often called a rotunda though ovaliform.

The north-south street in the inner courtyard of the Sheraton led off the main forum, which was situated in the central square now called Sveta Nedelya, or Holy Sabbath. Under the Christian church of St George lay a secular building which may have been erected as a *martyrion* (memorial temple), or a mausoleum, or even another baths-complex, suggested by the discovery of a hypocaust under the domed

Plan of the Romano-Byzantine Wall

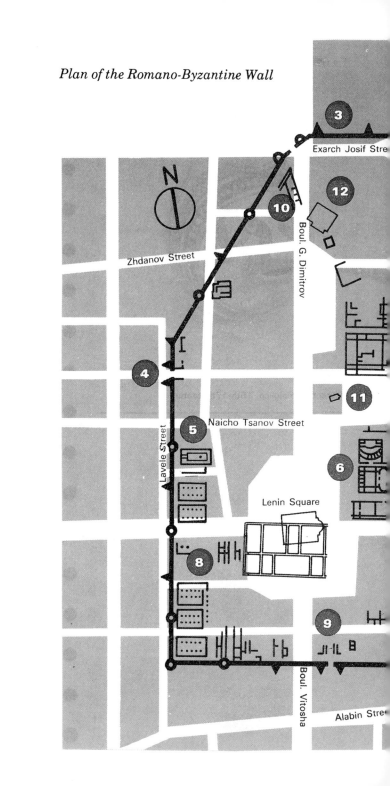

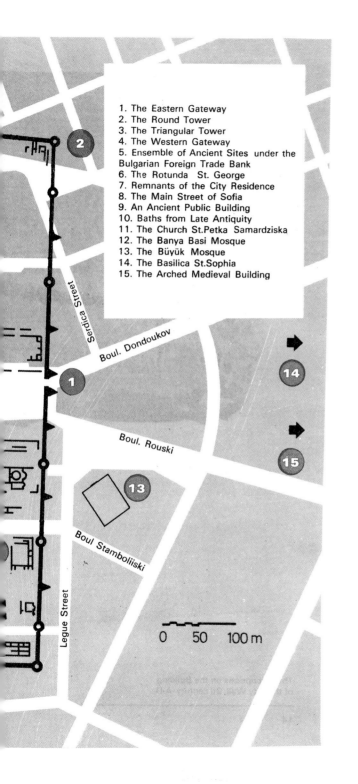

1. The Eastern Gateway
2. The Round Tower
3. The Triangular Tower
4. The Western Gateway
5. Ensemble of Ancient Sites under the Bulgarian Foreign Trade Bank
6. The Rotunda St. George
7. Remnants of the City Residence
8. The Main Street of Sofia
9. An Ancient Public Building
10. Baths from Late Antiquity
11. The Church St.Petka Samardziska
12. The Banya Basi Mosque
13. The Büyük Mosque
14. The Basilica St.Sophia
15. The Arched Medieval Building

Serdica Street

Boul. Dondoukov

Boul. Rouski

Boul Stamboliiski

Legue Street

0   50   100 m

chamber. While other buildings in Bulgaria of the 4th century have all been built over or demolished, St George emerges from the lower levels of history as solid as the saint in those iconostases that stubbornly revere his mystery as fact throughout the length and breadth of all Bulgaria. The symbol of the Christian saint slaying the infidel dragon would never be silent during all those grim centuries when Allah dictated to the Muslim conquerors that no human or animal image should be carved, painted or revered. Though it is evident on the ground that most of this elaborate complex was destroyed early on (during the 5th century, conceivably by Huns), the 'rotunda' was saved and decorated, though the first murals to survive are of the late 10th or early 11th century, and depict three of sixteen prophets that once stood guard, as well as eight vigorous angels in flight that soared above the heads of earnest worshippers. Saints are visible on the western wall beneath the frieze, all bearing Greek inscriptions. During the 12th century the church was redecorated, with Christ Pantocrator in the centre of the dome as is usual in Orthodox iconography, accompanied by his four Evangelists and four angels. Twenty-two standing figures of prophets proclaim the equivalence of Old Testament stories with New Testament revelations, Slavonic inscriptions above them emblematic of the Second Bulgarian Kingdom. Over the southern entrance the Assumption of the Blessed Virgin Mary is painted; above the northern, the Ascension of Christ: elsewhere vigorous brushwork, heavily restored for clarity, portrays the Nativity of Our Lord, the Purification of Mary, the Annunciation, Baptism, Transfiguration, and the Raising of Lazarus.

Selim I (1512-20) decreed that St George should become the Rose Mosque (Gül Cami), and a minaret called the faithful from its southwestern corner. The murals were not demolished, but overpainted in white, with the names of Allah and his Prophet (salla Allahu alayhi wa sallam) inscribed in blue, so that there should be no pictorial, blasphemous distraction from the name of God.

Църквата св. София – L'église de Sainte-Sophia *diese Kirche ist von Römischen Zeiten gebaut.*

Church of the Holy Wisdom in a postcard, c. 1910

Hagia Sophia, or Sveta Sofia in Bulgarian, hides modestly, a discreet maiden in a square fantastically dominated by the rich Russophile Alexander Nevski domes, isolated here as St Basil's is beyond Moscow's Kremlin walls. Wherever you look in Nevski Square, the modern memorial cathedral proclaims its spatial hegemony, while the faint syllables of Holy Wisdom are relegated to a leafy corner. But I know which I prefer.

The original church was erected as a *basilica sepulcralis*, or burial church, serving the adjacent city acropolis in the fourth century. An intricate mosaic with birds and trees from this time has been preserved in the Archaeological Museum (Büyük Cami). The Visigoths having demolished this church in the fourth century, it was restored and enlarged to three naves in the fifth, before Justinian's reign, but razed by invading Huns in 447. The present-day church also antedates Justinian, and may have been built rather quickly, on the same three-nave model, with a three-sided apse and cruciform dome over a transept. The central nave would have been three storeys high, one storey above the flanking naves.

This church was rebuilt during the Second Bulgarian Kingdom (12th to 14th centuries) when it assumed metropolitan rank and possessed its own seminary. Now it was painted with suitable iconography, later whitewashed over when converted into a mosque at the orders of Selim I, who added a minaret in the southwest corner. It must have given the Ottomans great satisfaction here as at Constantinople to change the foremost Christian place of worship into a mosque. Nearby, as in Istanbul, a caravanserai was established, and rooms for dervishes laid out. Earthquakes rocked the historic pile in 1818, then in 1858, so that it stood abandoned. In 1910 it resumed active worship and reconstruction, leisurely at times, has allowed the heart of Sofia to beat once more. If you look outside behind the apse, you will find uncovered brickwork in the neat garden. I found the right-hand nave open for worship but silent and empty, with a few flickering candles. I sat in gathering darkness and reenacted in my mind that siege of the Bulgarian ruler Khan Krum in 809, when he overcome the Byzantines of Serdica Ulpia and bestowed on the town its Slavonic name Sredets (*sreda* meaning 'middle', based on a misunderstanding of the origin of 'Serdica'). The Slavonic town managed to stave off Byzantine forces under 987 but fell to them eventually and became a Byzantine frontier-post from 1018 to 1186.

7: A NIGHT AMONG THE WATERMELONS

September in Bulgaria is the melon season. Even in Sofia. The best ones come from the Danube, around Lom, and whenever I see a watermelon and I am near a knife, I seize the chance like a tomcat at a mousehole.

Even without a knife it is possible to come to some arrangement. I had just emerged from the Stefan Makedonski Music Theatre from seeing Imre Kalman's *The Queen of Czardas* and saw a suspiciously green mound of heavy footballs behind barbed-wire netting, as if someone had invented a jail for delinquent melons. I approached the large, smiling, cigarette-smoking vendor. He was flicking ash over the pages of a Bulgarian translation of French sea stories.

'Have you one that is ripe now?'

He expanded body and arms into a conductor's *molto espressivo*. 'They are all exactly ripe.'

'Can I eat one here'

'Why not?'

The café on Bulevard Vasil Levski is not equipped as a restaurant, but someone rustled up a sharp knife and we set to, dividing slices among the clientele, all sipping black Turkish coffee in the balmy dark around round umbrella-shaded tables which enhanced the intimacy.

Over coffee and melon, Georgi the melon-seller confided his tale as if he had known me all his life.

'I like you: I think you tell me the truth. That is not so common. When I see it I am inspired and like to do just the same. My parents came from a village called Boizhinovtsi, a hundred kilometres from Lom', he began, 'and they came to Sofia in 1950 for a better life. My father, now deceased, drove a truck and my mother was a storekeeper until she retired. In

1970 I finished high school, spent the regulation two years doing military service when I learned to drive all kinds of heavy vehicles, then in 1972 began work as an ambulance driver with the emergency services. I stuck that out for two years, then joined the police in 1974. Thirteen years I worked for the police, but I had such a stupid boss that I couldn't stand it any more. During that time I began to study law in the evenings, but I couldn't finish the course because I had no motivation.

'I married in the mid-1970s and my daughter, born in 1976, now lives with her mother because I divorced in 1982 on grounds of incompatibility. If I marry again, it's *only* to a Western girl, preferably an American. They know how to appreciate Bulgarian men more than our women do.'

'Would you emigrate if you had the chance?'

'With a Democratic government, I will stay here, but if we get another Communist government, I shall fly 'like a bat out of hell', yes?'

'Where would you go?'

'Anywhere: the Dead Sea, the desert, the jungle.'

'But for preference?'

'New Zealand.'

'Because that's as far as you can get from the Communists?'

'You've struck the nail where it hurts.'

'So what did you do when you left the police?'

'What didn't I do? Sentry, nightwatchman, fetch-and-carryman, ratcatcher. Wherever someone wanted something done: I had to keep alive. Now, during the season, I am a melonseller by night. The melons are trucked here from the north by a private firm who hire girls to sell melons by day. You can't have a girl selling melons at night, so I come at nine p.m. and leave at eight a.m. Reading, dreaming, selling, talking, drinking coffee while the café stays open to keep awake. They give me forty leva a night, that's about two dollars. I sell an average of 30-40 leva of melons a night, but they get a nightwatchman for that too. In the daytime the girls can make

Georgi Bozhinov

600-800 leva a shift. Criminals don't come to steal money. Imagine, if anyone tries violence, I can kill him with a watermelon! For reading, I like *National Geographic Magazine*, books on popular archaeology like Troy, the Hittites, O. Henry, Mark Twain, P.G. Wodehouse now there's a man I could read for all life long. That Blandings Castle! That Jeeves and Wooster! That *Heart of a Goof!* That Mr Mulliner! He is a gentleman, English like you, very gentle because nobody made you into a bully. With five hundred years of tyranny by the Turks we all became the same thing. The gentleness was beaten out of us with clubs. Real clubs. Spiritual clubs. Political threats. Unspoken threats against your family. I have no ambition because I was taught as a policeman not to have opinions above my station. If you have a little yeast you can become a big loaf. But if you stick out like a nail you will be hammered back down.'

His sad, deep eyes explored mine restlessly in search of a common background, then turned away in evident pain.

'The worst crime of the Bulgarian Socialist Party is to have infiltrated our Opposition so that reforms are stifled. It is an absolute condition of radical change that the Communist Party be abolished here as it is in Russia. But they aren't going to do that, because too many Communists will remain in power, so I am afraid. Afraid of a civil war. A peaceful revolution towards true democracy will not work. To defeat the Communists we shall have to use their own ruthless methods. Purges, innuendoes, witch-hunts, show trials to convict those guilty of leading the country into our present morass. The Leninist method of brutal tyranny led to tragedy, and we have to reverse all the terrible results of those years in order to start afresh.'

'Will you democrats start the civil war?'

'No, because we have the ascendancy for the time being. The Communists will begin the civil war because they have the weapons, like *haiduts*. We shall have to overcome their insidious, sudden ambushes.'

'How do you describe the Bulgarian national character?'

'We are blighted by poor family upbringing, poor school education, poor public morality. We are simple people, but naturally intelligent. If we are just allowed for once to make our own luck we shall succeed, but so many obstacles have been put in our path in these past decades that we haven't had the chance to show what we can do. I believe in the American Declaration of Independence and all other democratic rights. I believe in the rights of man, the rights to a dignified life, to liberty, and the pursuit of whatever happiness you desire.'

Every evening, on my way home, I would stop off at Georgi's melon stall. We'd exchange the day's news, I'd tell him what I'd done, where I'd been, whom I'd seen. As we became ever closer, we'd throw our arms around each other affectionately, and the chats would go on longer. The café-owner would genially wave away my attempts to pay for coffee. Regular patrons would shake my hand and cluster round for gossip, introducing me to their friends and family. Urchins would squat beside our tables, gazing up in rapt attention at the peculiar foreign words spoken by the *anglichanin*. I still wonder what I had done to earn such attentive, delightful friends with their extended families.

And now the watermelon season is over? Georgi still writes. Sofia, 24 October 1992. 'Here everything is almost perfect. I'm without any work again, but I have an experience and after time everything will be alright. I'll be grateful forever to the fortune and to the watermelons, that I met you.' Here's to you, Zhoro!

8: OTTOMAN SOFIA

The Sofia ruled by Ivan Shishman fell to the Ottomans in 1382, and with the exception of a brief interregnum under the Hungarians led by Janos Hunyadi from 1443, it remained in Ottoman hands until 1878. The Ottoman Emperor's view of Sofia was that it constituted a strategic capital in which to establish a governor-general or *beylerbey* responsible for most of the Balkan Peninsula except the Morea and Bosnia.

Sofia's population increased, mainly as a result of immigration from Turkish-occupied lands. Records indicate that in 1553 Sofia boasted eleven large and up to a hundred small mosques. Understandably, Bulgarians nowadays seem reluctant to discuss or study this long period of their history, except insofar as Bulgarians can be portrayed as *haidut* defenders, *guerrilleros* of Che Guevara's charisma, who raided from the hillsides, only to disappear once more, like Robin Hood into Sherwood Forest.

The truth was more sombre: after the conquest of Constantinople in 1453, Bulgarian resistance was crushed. The state administration was abolished, privileges of the Bulgarian nobility swept away, and the Bulgarian Orthodox Church assigned to subservience under the Greek Patriarch. Monasteries were closed, churches weakened if not closed, and the intelligentsia forced to flee. Some Bulgarians preferred for good honest reasons of their own to convert as 'collaborators', which is the meaning of 'Pomaks'. Those who did not convert were given the status of *ahl adh-dhimma*, or 'people of the contract', that is to say those who did not accept Islam, but would be allowed to live in a Muslim state subject to fulfilling conditions of a kind of social contract. Hospitality and protection is afforded to 'peoples of the Book', that is Jews and Christians, subject to various stipulations, such as the payment of a *jizya* or poll-tax, and from time to time such demands as supplying provisions for an army, by observing prohibitions on wearing Arab dress, and above all by recognising the dominant faith.

Ottoman Sofia possessed a number of distinguished buildings for the use of Bulgarians, though they may seem in retrospect unpretentious to the point of humility. Many churches were converted into mosques, but towards the end of the 16th century the Muslim authorities relaxed their ban on the building of churches, and some three hundred were built or rebuilt. Regulations confined their dimensions and their height, which had to reach no farther than the top of adjacent houses, requiring not only their foundations to be well below ground level, but even their main door: the symbolism of descending below ground level to worship the Christian God was not lost on the sardonic rulers.

Contemporary Bulgarian homes looked poverty-stricken, glum with timber and clay, at first consisting of only one room, then two including a kitchen, and eventually three or more. But no ostentation of any kind would be permitted. Churches of this time scattered throughout Bulgaria include the Church of the Virgin at Bachkovo Monastery, SS Theodore Tiron and Theodore at Dobursko, Kremikovtsi, Alinski and Karlukovo monasteries, and the churches financed by wealthy merchants or guilds.

One such guild, the Saddlers', reconstructed at their expense the little church named for Sveta Petka and known as 'Samarjiiska', *samar* meaning 'saddle'. Its foundations belong to a much earlier church razed by the Muslims because of its proximity to their city centre. We first hear of Sveta Petka in a document of 1578, but the original sanctuary is dated archaeologically not later than the 14th century, and it remained in almost constant active use until 1948. Sv. Petka is an 11th century saint from a wealthy family of Epivados, on the Sea of Marmara. The Muslim authorities demanded a plain exterior, but within imposed no limit on artistic expression, with the result that the earliest frescoes (recently redated, later than in traditional accounts, to the 16th century) possess a decorative and expressive strength we recognise in the art of most repressed communities.

Sveta Petka's murals once covered the entire interior, depicting scenes from the Bible, prophets, Fathers of the Church, hermits and saints, and early martyrs. Sensitive restoration enables us to respond to mediaeval Bulgarian art as to similar Orthodox works in Greece and Russia: Christ's Presentation in the Temple, The Washing of the Feet, and

Mural (16th century), Sveta Petka Samarjiiska

The Last Supper each recalls a period of compulsive piety, when Biblical stories were available to the masses in only aural or visual form, due to impeded literacy and a paucity of manuscripts.

Later murals here can only hint at such passionate portrayal: the second period is exemplified by the head of St Simon Stylites at the west end of the northern wall. Nineteenth-century accretions can be dismissed. There is a move by ecclesiastical authorities to regain possession of this gem, so carefully tended by the secular body for the protection of national monuments, but of course this would be mistaken in every sense but the merely symbolic.

The decorator may have been one Pimen, whose murals remind one of those on Crete or Mount Athos, and they have been restored (1960s-1970s) to the same high level of excellence that restorers have provided from Pliska to Turnovo and Boyana. Sv. Ivan Rilski appears opposite the niche on

Sveta Petka Samarjiiska, with Mosque of Banya Bashi (background) and corner of TsUM (right)

the right of the apse, and the Prophet Elijah gesticulates towards his present and future listeners. The small single-naved church has a vaulted roof with a later narthex, semi-circular apse, two deep niches and two shallow blind niches.

Another church of the Ottoman period is that dedicated to St George in the monastery of Kremikovtsi, located 25 km northeast of Sofia, and due north of Kremikovski village, an area wrecked and polluted for decades to come by inappropriately rampant industrialisation, dictated to Bulgarian Communists by Soviet example. Kremikovtsi Monastery originally dated to the Second Bulgarian Kingdom, but it was devastated by the invading Ottomans, and restored about 1493 by the Boyar Radivoi of nearby Sofia in memory of his deceased children Todor and Dragana. A second donor (recorded in the second narthex) rebuilt and restored the church and added new frescoes in 1611, and a third obliged in 1672, indicating the tenacious longevity of Kremikovtsi Monastery, which was held in high esteem as a centre for manuscripts and scholarship, attested by the Kremikovski Gospels completed in 1497 on the orders of Kalevit, Bishop of Sofia. Other churches tend to possess stylistic unity, but at Kremikovtsi we can distinguish at least four different painters, probably from different traditions, to judge from the hieratic full-face fresco of St Helena and the angular, black-outlined vivacity of the Annunciation to St Anne, who is caught in mid-movement by an angel clearly anxious to pass the message on quickly and return to Heaven. Even more evocative is the Radivoi family group on the north wall of the narthex, their imploring arms nearly shoulder-high, confronting the viewer as Radivoi hands over the church to Bishop Kalevit.

Of the hundred or so mosques in every quarter built or converted from churches, we have seen the examples of St George and Hagia Sofia ('St Sophia' implies that wisdom is personified; 'Sveta Sofia' implies it first existed after the Bulgarian incursions). The Great Mosque, much more important than either, was a formidable square structure completed in 1494, its three central domes larger than its flanking six. The harmonious whole would have been located near a medreseh, or Islamic theological college, caravanserais, and administrative offices. The other major mosques to survive are the so-called Black Mosque built in 1528 during the reign of Suleiman I, now Sveti Sedmochislenitsi Church, and the Banya Bashi Mosque built in 1576 during the reign of Mehmet Pasha.

The Great Mosque has been preserved but not for worship. It is the National Archaeological Museum, situated on the corner of Bulevard Stamboliiski next to the Bulgarian National Bank, and open daily from 10-12 and 2-6 everyday but Monday, like most Bulgarian museums. The museum was established in 1879, but opened in 1892, and now has over a quarter of a million objects, very few of which can be shown. The building is quite inadequate for its purpose, and developments in museology have passed it by. It should of course be restored to its religious function, and a new building, modern

Büyük Cami (The Great Mosque), now the National Archaeological Museum (c. 1916)

43

in concept and layout, should be created, if possible uniting the functions of the Museum of the City of Sofia which so far exists only on paper.

Damagingly, even its most spectacular works of art are dwarfed by their surroundings, like a bird in a forest. Every opportunity is lost: there are no captions in other languages, no guidebooks, catalogues, postcards or tours, no background information or audiovisual aids. The collections are divided into four departments: Prehistory, Antiquity, the Middle Ages, and Coins and Medals. Objects from the Palaeolithic include implements of flint, basalt and andesite, and a cave-bear's fang pierced as an amulet by a Palaeolithic hunter 37,000 years ago in the Samuilitsa Cave II near Kunino in the district of Vratsa, the oldest recorded manmade artefact in the country. Finds from the Middle and Late Palaeolithic come from the Bacho Kiro Cave near Dryanovo and the Morovitsa Cave near the enchanting village of Glozhene.

Over 400 Neolithic burial mounds throughout Bulgaria date from the Neolithic, starting in the 6th millennium B.C. The most outstanding is Tell Karanovo, still being excavated by a joint Bulgarian-Austrian team from Salzburg and Nova Zagora, with results from such a long period that analogies with Troy have been mooted. Inscriptions from the 4th millennium antedate writing from Crete and Mycenaean Greece. Iron Age weapons and adornment are comparable with those in neighbouring countries.

Antiquity is represented by Greek sculpture in originals or copies including a Demeter from Oescus (Gigen), an Eros from Nicopolis ad Istrum, and a Resting Satyr from Riben (Pleven).

Mediaeval works reveal the incursions of the first Bulgarians to Pliska and Preslav, between the 7th and 10th centuries: their inscriptions document battles, treaties and regulations. Only a few of the 200,000 coins are on show, but look for the Thracian *derons* minted by the Deroni at the end of the 6th century B.C. and at the other end of the time-scale the Bulgarian gold, silver and copper coins minted by decree of Tsar Asen II (1218-41)

The second of our great Sofiote mosques, known from the colour of its granite as the Black Mosque, rises solid as the perennial *shahadatain*: 'God is Great and Muhammad is God's Prophet'. It can be found where Ulitsa Graf Ignatiev meets Ulitsa Tsar Shishman, near the bookstalls of Slaveikov Square. Dating from 1528, it has been converted into a church dedicated to the Holy Apostles, literally the 'Number Sevens' (*sedmo*-seven; *chislen*-number), that is to say Cyril and Methodius with five disciples: Kliment of Ohrid, after whom Sofia University is named, Naum, Gorazd, Sava and Angelairi. Sultan Suleiman the Magnificent was responsible for many such mosques; it reminds me of those in Bursa and Edirne. The Russians who captured Sofia from the Ottomans in 1878 used the mosque as a weapons store, then the Russian architect A.N. Pomerantsev was asked to create within the original framework a new Orthodox Church. The Bulgarian architects Petko Momchilov and Yordan Milanov took the responsibility for day-to-day administration, and icons were painted by Anton Mitov and Stefan Ivanov. Sensitivity prevailed, so that of the mosque virtually nothing was destroyed: the only alterations are the porch and two wide doors of 1901-3.

Two old ladies, sisters or neighbours, kissed an icon of Our Lord, and stuck flickering candles in a circular candle-holder. An old lady in a blue cardigan pulled out dying candles, blew them definitively out, and padded back to the main door where she would sell more such hostages to time. I felt an intruder as the ladies stood and prayed to the Christian God in this magnificent mosque.

Kara Cami's minaret is demolished, like those of Gül Cami (St George) and Siaush Cami (Holy Wisdom), but a gracious minaret is to be seen in the heart of tolerant Sofia, within a stone's throw of the Synagogue. It belongs to the mosque known as Banya Bashi because it is situated close to the baths, or 'banya' in Bulgarian. Erected in 1576, it has an arcade of four columns, three elegant entrance domes and a huge central dome mimicking the sky above. To the right of the mihrab or niche facing Makkah al-Mukarramah is the name of Allah in gold on a black circle. Muhammad's name appears on the left, then Abu Bakr, Uthman, Hasan, Husain, Ali and Umar. The wooden minbar or pulpit is inscribed on the arch at the foot of the steps *bismillahi ar-Rahman ar-Rahim,* 'in the name of God the Compassionate and Merciful.' The ablutions area remains open and had clearly been used recently. Rush mats were rolled up in niches. A wooden gallery hung above the entrance door; a tiled platform had been raised above the floor at each side of the door. A Muslim told me that the call to prayer by the muaddin had resumed a little while before, but 'it was made apparent' that such a call would be considered provocative to the Christian majority and, as at Shumen, the initiative had died. But surely in a tolerant society like newly-democratic Bulgaria, it would not offend anyone but the rabid fanatic whose opinions should hardly govern our lives? Unfortunately the old Ottoman baths no longer exist, having been replaced by Petko Momchilov's impressive neo-Renaissance monument finished in 1913, and currently closed for restoration.

The Ottomans cannily recruited administrators from all over their vast Empire, from Albania to Egypt, on the principle of 'divide and rule', and allowed trade to be managed by Armenians, Jews, and Greeks and merchants from Dubrovnik dealing with western Europe and Venice. The Greeks governed church life, schools, and writing generally, dismissing the study of Bulgarian to the home and earth, as Turkish and Romany were relegated in Communist Bulgaria. A levy of young Bulgarian boys was taken from each community for instruction and conversion before being recruited into the élite corps of Janissaries.

Oppression of the Bulgarian Orthodox Church by absorption into the Greek Orthodox Church made education and historiography very difficult, but seventeenth-century Bulgarian Catholics drew attention to their country and its past. Petur Bakshev, Catholic Bishop of Sofia, wrote an *Opisanie*

Central Mineral Baths (1913)

na Bulgarsko Tsarstvo (1640) and a history of Bulgaria (1668), while Petur Parchevich achieved high rank in the Vatican, but Catholic influence in Bulgaria ended with the disastrous revolt of 1688.

In the 18th century Father Païsi of the Hilendar monastery on Mount Athos wrote an enthusiastic anti-Greek history of Bulgaria from the Orthodox viewpoint in a language mixing Church Slavonic with a more modern idiom, enjoining his readers to cultivate their language and their history. Further advances were made by Sofroni of Vratsa, in a racier Bulgarian, extending the range of conversational Bulgarian to a literary level in *Nedelnik* (Bucharest, 1806). Gerhard Driesch, a German traveller, could write in 1790 that 'Sofia is one of the most beautiful cities in Turkey', but in 1793 the feudal ruler of Vidin, Osman Pazvantoghlu, descended with his horde on Sofia and ravaged the town. From its status as capital of Rumelia's *beylerbey* it sank to the status of a *sanjak* county town subservient to Ruse. The initiative and the opportunity for Sofia to rise again had been provisionally lost. The first modern school teaching in Bulgarian opened in Gabrovo in 1835, and throughout the land in the 1830s a new prosperity came from increased tolerance in the Ottoman Empire, social changes felt bracing, and economic progress occurred when Bulgarians were allowed to supply the new regular Ottoman army with food and cloth, then in the 1840s the ban on exporting wheat was abolished. Local guilds funded scholarships for young men to study abroad: they returned to teach in the two thousand free schools set up by the 1870s. Many of them urged on their compatriots the kind of autonomy that Serbia and Greece had won by 1830.

9: LUNCH AT A SELF-SERVICE

I had spent an hour in the Sheraton lounge waiting for a poet who didn't ever show up. A cup of tea cost 30 leva (roughly one pound sterling), a cappuccino 40 leva, and an Irish coffee 150 leva. A beautiful girl resembling the actress Billie Whitelaw (radiant, humorous, knowing, sensuous) asked me mock-deferentially if I wanted a drink, and I ruefully suggested waiting for my contact.

Across the lounge I had been listening to a huddle of twin Bulgarians and twin Italians speaking of business in measured, serious tones. *Seriozno,* 'seriously', is a word held in high esteem by Bulgarians, and these *mafiosi* in decorous tones seemed to exemplify its quasi-ironic tone.

That word jogged my memory of a smokefilled, crowded, noisy apartment on Angel Kunchev Street during the last days of the Zhivkov regime. We had all drunk too much during a hilarious evening with a leading Bulgarian actor and his adoring fans. He had taken many lovers during the course of a distinguished and passionate career, and gently ridiculed my lifelong devotion to the woman I had married after a long and often apparently fruitless courtship. To a libertine, few men seem more foolish than a constant husband. Seriously!

'Take my advice,' he urged, striking the table with his open palm, 'if you fall in love with a woman in Sofia, seduce her the first day. If you wait to the second day, she will think you are indecisive. If you wait to the third day, she will know you are playing hard to get. If you wait till the fourth day...'

'Yes?'

'It will be too late; she will have been seduced by another man. *Seriozno!*'

I abandoned my appointment and sought solace in a cheap

Inside a Self-Service Restaurant near TsUM

lunch at a drab, dingy *self* near the Sofia Shop, not far from the elegant minaret of Banya Bashi mosque, while trams clanked and braked past.

As a small child or wartime and utility Britain I had taken cheap meals with my mother in a British Restaurant, with its sad, standard, limited fare. Those memories of overboiled cabbage and shabby tables, tired cooks and wrinkled shoppers, came back to haunt me here. Weak beer stood ready to put on your tray. I tried one glass, with a small bread roll, boiled cabbage and mutton, totalling 13.6 leva, or about US$0.75. I sat at a table laid with patched and torn blue cotton cloth. Hungry passers-by entered and, instead of begging, gazed around at trays of food left by previous eaters. Compassionate ladies uniformed in blue turned a blind eye to these intruders: is it not better to wolf the last scrap off a plate? Before eating, one was invited to use one of two sinks inside the door, only one of which still wore its tap.

A young man of 25 came and sat down beside me.

'You speak English?' 'I do, and you?'

'It is my whole life. But don't talk while you're eating. It is very bad.' I obediently held my peace until our plates sat clean.

'I lived for five months with a Baptist family in Newport, South Wales. I told them, "Never talk during a meal." Afterwards, they told me, "Thank you very much for your suggestion, it's much better this way."'

'Did you give them any other suggestions?'

'Yes, I gave my mottoes in English. These are, number one, first give in order to receive; number two, do whatever you want, but only try not to hurt innocent people.'

'These sound good plans. May I know your name and background?'

'Yes, I am called Ludmil Dimitrov Spasov and I used to be a sailor in the Bulgarian Navy, based in Varna. Now I live in Radomir and take the bus to Sofia to take English classes here. I think English, speak English, read English, write English. It is my way of escaping from the terrors of Communism. A Baptist family allowed me to escape for some months. I went to the Home Office and said, what should I do? I want to live always in England. They said, if you apply for political asylum and you are refused, you will never be able to come back to England for any reason. But if you don't apply, you can come back any time by invitation. They told me I had no grounds for requesting asylum. So I thought, better not to apply. But I am still in agony over that decision, because I am never invited back. Could you invite me back?'

'I don't really know what I can do. I am a writer: I don't employ anyone.'

'Here is my address. If you know anyone in Canada who could invite me, just let them have this.'

'Very well.'

We shook hands and he left with a parting wave.

'Or Australia.'

A scholarly-looking, stooping, bearded blue-overalled man

51

in his early thirties slowly cleared trays away from the cracked marble-topped tables.

A man in his early forties in a T-shirt overprinted UTOPIA entered guiltily from the sunny pavement, scanned dishes abandoned by departed diners, found three bits of bread rolls, and scooped them all on to one tray. Sitting bolt upright on a stool, he chewed them defiantly, head high, like someone who has paid for his meal.

As I emerged from the restaurant, a group of youths lounged insolently around a spick-and-span van bearing the name *Narodna Milicja*, 'People's Army'. One yelled to an officer, 'Why doesn't it just say "Army"?'

'What's wrong with "Police"?' shouted another. 'Ah, break it up,' spat a third. 'What's it matter? Call them what you like, they're still the same thugs.'

I smiled insincerely at a foreign woman retailing Krishna Consciousness books and posters on the pavement. At least she, on her own, had the courage of her convictions in the milling crowd. Young American male Mormons jostled together for protection, sweating with apprehension lest they were roughed up by a crowd of gipsies laughing with excess beer.

10: THE GROWTH OF A CAPITAL

Emerging from the Ottoman period at the period of S. Amadier's new town plan, Sofia's population in 1879 was roughly 12,000, rising to 20,500 in 1881 and 30,428 in 1888. In 1890 a modernised water-supply infrastructure encouraged further immigration: the population in 1893 had risen to 46,593.

The Eagles' Bridge and Lions' Bridge (1891) by the Czech Prošek mark the entrances to the city from south and north; at the Eagles' Bridge Bulevard Lenin meets Bulevard Ruski and at Lions' Bridge Dimitrov meets Slivnitsa. London is divided by the Thames, Paris by the Seine, but Sofia blithely disregards its two little rivers, the Vladaya, which marked the city's northern limit in 1879, and the Perlova, both tributaries of the Iskur.

София. Циганския кварталъ

The Gipsy Quarter, c. 1912

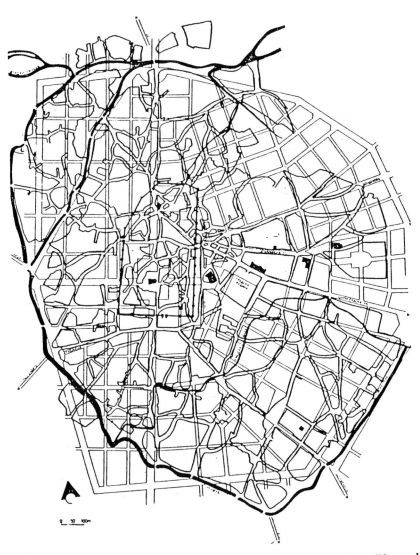

The Roman city (central rectangle), the historic centre in 1879, and the town plan by S. Amadier approved in 1880

In 1900, the old romantic but largely inefficient gaslighting was replaced by electric lighting: the population was 68,000.

Bulevard Marie-Louise (c. 1916), later renamed Bul. Evlogi Georgiev and Bul. Bulgaria

The tram system began in 1901, permitting even the poorest workers to become mobile, and in 1907 the population had soared to 82,187; in 1910 to 103,000.

The Balkan wars and the wars in Europe disrupted life in Sofia as in other Central European capitals, but in 1934 the capital territory had expanded to 42 square km and its population to 287,095. A decree of 1934 inaugurated the second Sofia City Plan, a bold projection which forms the basis of the current City Plan with its underground railway, to consist of three lines pragmatically linking the major conurbations in Greater Sofia. At the end of World War II, in 1946, the population stood at 436,936; in 1956 it had risen to 644,727, and in 1986 to 1.1 million.

Modern monumental Sofia up to the demise of Communism in 1989 had been constructed to a great extent by teams of architects. The group led by Vasilyov and Tsolov were responsible for the Bulgarian National Bank, the Ministry of

Defence, the National Library of SS. Cyril and Methodius (1942-54), and the University Library. The Belkovski-Danchov group created the German School, and the Hotel Bulgaria with the Bulgaria Concert Hall. The Fingov-Yurukov-Nichev group designed the French-Bulgarian Bank, the Bulgarian Commercial Bank, and the Phoenix Insurance building.

Reinforced concrete began to inch its way ever more insistently into Sofia as huge numbers of immigrants demanded quickly available housing, but at the expense of

The National Library (1942-54)

ever poorer standards. The Mussmann plan of the 1930s (which projected a population of only 600,000 by 1984) had to be drastically revised; as early as 1945-9 the Tonev plan showed dramatic changes, largely to accommodate hundreds of thousands of new workers for new industries on the Soviet model dictated by Party bosses. This plan too fell victim to ideological changes, and in 1961 a new plan was based on the work of the Neikov and Siromahov groups. Smaller prewar hotels gave way to enormous hotel complexes with international participation. Smaller factories gave way to gigantic state enterprises. Creeping urbanization was followed by the demolition of rural districts for massive apartment blocks, as at Lyulin and Mladost, each the size of a small town. A university students' town was knocked up rapidly to meet ever-increasing demands for higher education. To give some idea of the rush, only 3,323 apartments were built in the period 1949-52, but in the 1970s it was quite usual to build up to 15,000 apartments in one year. In 1975 Bulevard Lenin was reconstructed as a multi-lane dual carriageway, giving downtown access from the airport within twenty minutes.

Typical instances of modern architecture of this period in-clude the Television Tower (1959-60) by L. Popdonev, Univer-siad Hall (1961) by the A. Barov group, Hotel Pliska (1965) by Hr. Tsvetkov and L. Lozanov, L. Pindeva's Serdika Hotel (1967) near the Vasil Levski Monument, A. Barov's Grand Hotel Sofia (1969), Zlatev and Rangelov's Hotel Hemus (1969-70), I. Kavalov group's Union of Bulgarian Artists on Ulitsa Shipka (1969-70) and L. Popdonev's Ministry of Trans-port (1970).

When I spoke to Belin Mollov, Director of the City Plan for Sofia in the 1990s, he pointed out that for the first time the Local Government Law of 17 September 1991 allocated him his own city budget independent of the central state bureau-cracy. Expansion of the city of more than one million, con-taining more than a ninth of the country's population, will be to the southwest and southeast, within the existing territory of Greater Sofia. When the old apartment-block districts of Mladost and Druzhba come to the end of their natural lives, in ten or twenty years, they will be replaced by individual homes and gardens.

Architect Mollov explained, 'We shall not make the same mistake, like the Hippodrome Housing Estate (1957-60) or the Dimitrov District (B5, of 1976), which is totalitarian in concept, design, and in the cynical use of shoddy building materials. I am not going to predict any future architectural style, for the simple reason that we shall offer projects to tender by a large number of small private architectural practices, each with its own idiosyncrasies. Our major transport innovation in the 1990s will be the Sofia City Metro system, with three lines meeting in the centre, and reaching all points of the compass.

Line 1 will begin at Obelya, coming from Lyulin and Western Park to Vuzrazhdane, Sveta Nedelya in the centre, to Orlov Most and Mladost. This will serve 150,000 people in Lyulin and at least 200,000 in Mladost. Line 2 will start in the north at Ilientsi industrial zone, and link the Central Rail Station with Lions' Bridge, Sveta Nedelya junction, National Palace of Culture, Hotel Vitosha New Otani, and Lozenets. Line 3 will begin at Gorna Banya, touching Bulevard Makedonia, the centre, Poduene, Bulevard Misia, and ending at Levski, near the Airport. The whole network is 52 km long, but of course can be extended in all directions.

Sofia's motto is 'Raste, no ne staree', which signifies 'It grows, but doesn't grow old', obviously referring to the fact that centuries of neglect, before the city became national capital in 1879, had done little for Sofia's self-respect, but its rapid growth during the past century had seemed to rejuvenate the spirit of the place.

11: MIDNIGHT ON THE SQUARE

Lenin Square, now bereft of its Lenin statue, has been re-named Holy Sabbath Square for its dominant church. On one side is the Sofia University Faculty of Theology built by Petko Momchilov in 1900-5. On another side the Sheraton Hotel, with its fabulously expensive suites, payable in hard currency, squats like a capitalist frog in a Bulgarian pond. Beyond its frontiers, its serried ranks of hopeful taxis, girls emerge to strut after nightfall.

Everybody was smoking. They puff away, they chain-smoke, they live in a haze of coughing fumes. Even the doctors smoke, the surgeons, nurses and medical students. I wouldn't bet against the lung-cancer patients being able to light up in the corridors.

Sofia University Faculty of Theology (1900-5)

My friend Todor, the taxi-driver, summoned a girl into the more decorous seclusion of his back seat, and explained that I sought only the gratification of noncarnal knowledge.

'I hope that men will always be rich and pathetic,' he translated for her. 'So that we can earn huge amounts from their arrogant and overwhelming desires. I am a single mother abandoned by my husband, and I have three children. The government's allowance for three children is not enough for them to eat properly, so I leave them with my mother while I come out to work. She has never asked me a question. She just cries.'

'These men think they are attractive, but for choice I would not be seen in a restaurant with one in a hundred of the men who come to me. With a foreign tour group of eight businessman I can make sixty dollars each for a whole night, that's nearly five hundred dollars. For a Bulgarian woman working in a shop, that's nearly a year's salary earned in one night's work. My pimp gets a lot of course, to protect me from other pimps, but in a regular job I should see my family starve, honourably. Which is the moral woman: the one who feeds her children or the one who starves them?'

'It is so nice to talk with a reasonable man like you who treats me as a human being. Why can't other men pay me just for talking, and listening, and being together for companionship and friendship and warmth and love? I hate sex, because it makes me a slave. No, I don't like what I do, but in this country the women earn the money and the men spend it. The government consists of men, and they make sure our income in leva is not enough so we go out and earn hard currency for them. I do not act with dignity, but I think with dignity: that you cannot see. Other women had to settle for even less, under Communism. Women used to go with party bosses for nothing, just because of blackmail, so their husbands and brothers and sons would not suffer. Why should we wait any longer, for our financial liberation? If the foreigners want to pay us for this and this only, let us be rich.'

'No, you can't take my photo, because one day soon I'll stop this life and become a shop-owner and a little housewife, with a little shopping bag and children who look up to me as a proper mother. I don't want to be remembered in such a photograph.'

'By the way, if you don't want to spend an hour with me, my boy-friend would like to change your money, yes?'

12: NATIONAL HISTORY MUSEUM

Encased in its strait-jacket of a neo-classical Palace of Justice (1926), Bulgaria's premier museum may suffer from unsuitable premises (reconstructed in 1981-3), but one quickly forgets such inconveniences in the extraordinary quality of its Thracian treasures: Vulchitrun, found in 1924; Duvanli Galitsa (1938), Panagyurishte (1949), Lukovit (1953), Letnitsa (1963), Mogilanska (1965), Yakimovo (1972), Borovo (1974) and Rogozhen (Vratsa, 1985) the latest and in some ways the most spectacular silver hoard of all, with 54 jugs, 3 goblets and 108 plates and dishes fit for any royal feast. Dated variously to the 5th or the first half of the 4th century B.C., the objects are gilded by notable silversmiths, and have motifs both engraved and in relief. Greek myths and fabulous beasts; scenes of the hunt and depictions of Helios, the Sun-God, a lion pouncing on a stag and winged sphinxes. Who is to say where the next hoard will be uncovered, and what new artistic treasures will emerge?

The museum's central hall opens with the glorious 9th-century ceramic icon of St Theodore from Preslav, brilliantly restored. Objects from more than 170 graves in Varna's Chalcolithic Necropolis of around 4,000 B.C. whet our appetite for a visit to the Black Sea city's own museum. Finds come from Durankulak near Dobrich (the former Tolbuhin), and Roman mosaics from Ivailovgrad near Kurjali. A bronze head of Gordian III represents the best objects from Nicopolis ad Istrum (referring to the Danube; Nicopolis ad Nestrum is the modern Gotse Delchev, near the southwest border). Copies of Pliska columns reused in a later Bulgarian capital, Veliko Turnovo, stand near the Panagyurishte gold hoard. A silver-gilt breastplate comes from Mezek (southeast Bulgaria), whose corridor tomb and false vault resembles that at Kazanluk. Madara's pagan sanctuaries preceded the first Christian churches; here too is an appliqué with gryphon from royal Preslav, and ivory from Turnovo. An episcopal throne from Rila Monastery dates from the 14th century and a newly exhibited bronze cross bears the name of Sevast Borislav (12th-13th centuries). Two lively peacocks in red schist (10th-11th centuries) come from Stara Zagora.

National History Museum, Bul. Vitosha

National History Museum. Thracian gilded silver rhyton with sphinx relief from Borovo (4th century B.C.)

Dazzled for the moment by these high points, we begin the systematic sequence with the prehistoric age. Wonders include engraved tablets from Ovcharovo which have led scholars to assume that they are attempts at writing dating as far back as 6,500 years B.C., and small ritual altars of the same approximate age from Hotnitsa near Vratsa. The Chalcolithic or Copper Age (4th-3rd millennia) is extraordinarily rich in Bulgaria, and the Bronze Age (3200-1200 B.C.) scarcely less so, but it is with the Iron Age of the second millennium B.C. and the rich material culture of the Thracian tribes that we emerge on to the light of historic day. We can visit their hundreds of burial mounds today, and marvel at their golden treasure of Vulchitrun; their pre-Christian folklore is preserved in Kukeri or masked mumming rituals timed for the end of winter in festivals as far-flung as Pernik and Yambol, Plovdiv and Razlog, Elhovo and Radomir.

Documents show that Thracians exported corn, wax, timber, wool and hides to Greece in exchange for olive oil, silks and other fabrics. Protobulgars from the East intermarried with southern Slavic tribes of Moesia and Thrace, giving rise to the First Bulgarian Kingdom of Khan Asparuh in 681, and the Golden Age of Simeon I. Paganism makes way for Christianity, and the domination of Byzantium (1018-1186) ends with the Second Bulgarian Kingdom proclaimed at Veliko Turnovo. The Glagolitic alphabet is created by Cyril and Methodius, then modified by Kliment of Ohrid and others, the latest changes to Bulgarian Cyrillic coming in the 1940s, bringing it virtually into line with Russian Cyrillic, though Bulgarian sounds more melodious (the harsh *shch* of Russian is missing; the frequent Russian *ye* is simplified to *e*). Historic manuscripts and inscriptions on stone and brick evoke that distant past when Christianity would be spread in precious single copies of the Gospels, in books of hours, sermons, hymns. When writing belonged to priests and monks, each book was a treasure, like this 11th-century manuscript from Rila, or the 13th-century Gospels of Priest Dobreisho open at the miniature of St John the Evangelist.

On the upper floor, the Ottoman Period is represented by the rise of new towns such as Pazarjik, Kotel and Zheravna, the resurrection of peninsular Nesebur, and such monasteries as Kremikovtsi restored by the Sofiote boyar Radivoi with the support of the then Bishop of Sofia, Kalevit, in the 15th century. The goldsmith Georgi achieved canonisation as the New St George when burned at the stake in 1511 for his refusal to renounce Christianity. The New St Nikola of Sofia was stoned to death four years later. Such persistence of faith is exemplified by religious art of the 16th century from Turnovo, by murals from Nesebur, icons from Bachkovo, and books and icons brought from Etropole Monastery, including Four Gospels of the 16th century with a splendid Celtic-style interweaving pattern opposite a portrait of St Luke. One room is aptly devoted to the zenith of Bulgarian monasticism, Rila, exemplified by a MS of 1483 and the Iconostasis of St Luke (1779). Restored Samokov-school icons accompany self-portraits of Zahari Zograf (1840-2) and Dimitur Dobrovich (1875-80).

Remember that the museum is closed every Monday.

13: THE PASSION OF J.S. OBERBAUER

If you had strolled the streets of Sofia during the 1890s, you might as well have encountered at weekends and on summer evenings an earnest Austrian in his 40s from the Alpine town of Sankt Leonhard, sketching scenes of markets, churches, mosques and bridges, dense with life and colour. He was not a visitor, tourist, or traveller: he worked for the Town Hall as a construction specialist, on the first city plan of liberated Sofia.

Sofia through the eyes of Joseph Sebastian Oberbauer still looks Ottoman, with its minarets and ramshackle caravanserais, cobbled streets and open-air butchers' shops. Through these sixty-odd watercolours and drawings in the Museum of the City of Sofia, we see the Black Mosque as it was when Ulitsa Graf Ignatiev was still known as the Samokov Road, and an onion-domed high stone clock-tower overshadowed the area between Ul. Malko Turnovo and Ul. Moskovska. Fountains and narrow twisting streets, vaulted bridges and spirited markets fascinated the middle-aged Austrian, who had studied engineering at Graz before abandoning his career to become an artist, a profession he couldn't follow because of lack of means. Instead he became a teacher until 1889 when he moved to Sofia as one of the many Central Europeans recruited by the young free state. After the city plan was completed he took a job in the department for railways and ports but returned to the Town Hall to finish his working career there; he died in Sofia in 1926.

In the loving detail of topographical masterpieces such as 'Street with Slivnishki Inn', Oberbauer displayed that passion for Bulgaria which unites foreigners from all over the world who have skied on Borovets or wandered around the magical royal garden at Balchik, once the Queen of Romania's hideaway from the world's tumult. After Innsbruck, Sofia must have seemed exotically oriental, yet after Sankt Leonhard the snowy heights of Vitosha may have struck him as strikingly familiar. He drew wood-carved ceilings, Turkish boys with their mongrels, old ladies outside the centrally-located Church of St George, arcaded against sun and rain, but tiled glowing red, like any simple house of the time.

Oberbauer is at his genial best in portraying the lives of everyday folk, preoccupied with shopping perhaps, or chatting in a group outlined against Banya Bashi mosque. Yoked bullocks bring a load to the Grain Market near Ulitsa Iskur; neighbours squat on the cobbled kerb with their baskets, while a shopkeeper sweeps it clean with a long brush. In a precious view of the Turkish konak, later Royal Palace, now in a different guise as a modernised National Art Gallery, the dignified exterior is shamed by a plebeian white fence tailing off like an actor forgetting his lines. The essence of Oberbauer is not originality for its own sake, but an endearing passion for the ordinary life of Sofia. 'Look', he says to us, 'the sun rises on another day below the heights of Vitosha. What could be more awe-inspiring in the grand scale, what more intimate on the human scale?'

Watercolours of Sofia in the 1890s by Oberbauer: Graf Ignatiev's House (top); Belopopski Inn (centre); and Inn in Ulitsa Lomska

14: BOURGEOIS HOMES

Let nobody tell you that Sofia's housing is confined to 'Brave New World' uniformity. If you know where to look, gracious houses, patrician or petit bourgeois, can be found in many quarters, like the Dimitrov quarter, once known as Yuchbunar, an enclave of prosperous Jews now almost to a man dispersed through Israel and the diaspora. Many of the finest mansions were converted effortlessly into embassies; others were destroyed in air-raids, or have fallen victim to road-widening, the requirements of socialist construction on the normal superhuman or megalomaniac scale typified in the Largo, which dates from 1952 to 1955. Many Sofiotes still defend such gigantism fiercely, because they were brought up with it. If you were brought up in the home of E. Chaprašikova (1931-2) by I. Vasilyov and D. Tsolov, on the other hand, you might have regretted such monumentalism. This home can be found at 48 Bulevard Klement Gottwald, and now houses the Polish Commercial Representation. How admirable too are the exteriors of the Moroccan Embassy at 44 Gottwald and the Kuwaiti Embassy at No. 47! The glorious external details of the Hotel Imperial (1920) or of Nikola Lazarov's Gendovič Building (1914); the fine proportions of the Adolf Funk House (1910), now accommodating the Bulgarian Red Cross, and the refined flamboyance of K. Heinrich's 1912 house for R. Goranov, all speak of a national romanticism which was never afraid to borrow Viennese glories, classical columns and even caryatids in the case of the 1910 Central Cooperative Bank (1910), with an extra storey added in 1920, now the State Savings Bank headquarters.

You could start at the National Library, strongly classical in feeling despite the clashing huge figures of Cyril and

Methodius (Vladimir Ginovski, 1975), looming against the skyline like brooding giants, Fasolt and Fafner before being metamorphosed into dragons. On one side of the National Library runs Ulitsa Shipka, named for the Balkan pass which saw epic struggles (1877-8) between Ottoman forces and Russo-Bulgarian men. On the other, Ulitsa Oborishte also joins Bulevard Gottwald, and still retains its seclusion within high stone walls, locked gates, and darkened rooms, for these are patrician houses made over in some cases to embassies. Ulitsa Oborishte 27 is a most delightful residence, not sur-

Nikola Lazarov's House (now the French Embassy), Ul. Oborishte 27

71

prisingly created by an architect, Nikola Lazarov, for his own use, in restrained French neo-Baroque. The Spanish Embassy is situated at no. 47, and at number 10 (next door to the Residence) is the office of the Libyan People's Bureau, which is Muammar al-Qaddafi's jargon for Embassy.

Ulitsa Shipka has embassies too (Italy at no. 2 and Switzerland at no. 35), but it is dominated by two enormous institutions: Ivo Tsolov and Georgi Berberov's House of Soviet Science and Culture, which may become a white elephant in these post-Union times, and at number 6 the Art Gallery of the Union of Bulgarian Artists (1972) by Ivan Kavalov and Ivan Nikolov, which may flourish more vibrantly in future days after the collapse of the socialist realism dogma.

The Doctors' Garden, with a Doctors' Monument of 1883, is dedicated to all nursing, medical and surgical personnel who fell in the Russo-Turkish War of Liberation. A lapidarium in the corner of the garden off Ulitsa San Stefano looks as if the archaeological museum had lost some trophies through a hole in a sack. Here is a Muslim tombstone, there a fallen column fragment, yonder a barely decipherable inscription: *o tempora, o mores.* Nobody stopped but I, not even an inquisitive dog looking for a handy tree. Pedestrians hurried by, motorists swished past even faster, all caught up like dead leaves in a whirlwind present which acknowledges no valid history. Though nobody in Sofia ever asked me such a question as I explored its secrets street by street, I recalled that irate mansion-dweller in Jaipur some years ago who saw me measuring a haveli balcony: 'Is se faida kya hoga?' – 'What do you think you will gain by this?', to which I was not quick enough to respond: 'Another dimension: time'. We are all aware of living in the present and planning for the best possible future, but this should involve a detailed and sympathetic understanding of the past, both our own and that of everyone else, if we practise E.M. Forster's wisdom to 'only connect'.

On my 1947 map of Sofia in the Militsionersko Delo *Putevoditel na Sofia,* Ulitsa 3 April is named Ulitsa Yosif Broz Tito, yet another example of socialist countries' constantly switched street-names, building-names, and opinions according to the prevailing *idée fixe*. Sometimes such changes are concealed behind an elaborate façade, sometimes they are announced to reverberating trumpets, old idols are demolished, new statues raised, but nothing ever lasted because nothing was based on true, eternal, or spiritual values. Margarita Koeva remembered not only when Ulitsa 3 April had been christened Ulitsa Marshal Zhdanov, but even earlier, when it had been called Ulitsa Pirotska, for the good and sensible reason that it led towards the village of Pirot.

Unlike the recent high-rise apartment blocks intended to house production units, as one communist organ memorably described human beings, the homes for merchants and petits bourgeois on Ulitsa 3 April are recognisably intended for real people. They are big enough for privacy and parties, with high ceilings for philosophical conversation to hang long in the air, with a room set aside for a grand piano, and even a musical evening for friends. They are big enough for a cabinet of curiosities, for a private library, for an artist's studio. The library would have grandfather's leatherbound sets from Berlin and Frankfurt, father's clothbound volumes from Vienna and Munich, and the son's paperbacks from London and Paris – the Tauchnitz Library for railway travellers, souvenir albums from the Hermitage and the Pushkin Museum.

The best place to start is the splendid House of Lawyers, or Jurists as they are known in Bulgaria, which has its own modest chamber theatre and upstairs a club-restaurant open nightly to eleven. It dates from 1925-8, a fine period for Sofiote housing.

Most houses on 3 April are multifunctional, designed as shops on the ground floor, with store-rooms or warehouses at the back and spacious living quarters above. Now all of these gracious homes have been divided and subdivided into cramped flats, overcrowded and often noisy and poorly (because communally) maintained. An exception is number 10, pinkwashed to highlight the unobtrusive white decorative

73

columns and charming white window-frames. Number 16 (1911) is again subdivided into smaller apartments with jealous and suspicious residents who look as though they might, in an earlier age, have turned out slopbowls over an intruder's carefree head. 'What does he want?' called out a harridan in a brown overall. 'He *wants*,' replied Margarita Koeva, 'to admire your beautiful accommodation', and the crone banged shut her casement, well beaten. Number 16 seems evocative of those days immediately before the first Balkan War began in 1912 when life in Sofia seemed on the rise. The long, narrow courtyard opens into several shops, each with accommodation above at one time connected with the businesses but now sorrily separate: a clash of interests and personalities when one longs for the commonalty of Damascus spice-market or Bahrain gold suq, where you can leave your shop unattended because nobody will touch it and everybody will defend it from outsiders. All of these apartments were seized by the Communist Government in 1948 by the inequitably monstrous Law Concerning Private Property.

Ulitsa 3 April 15 (1911) has a dowdy knitwear shop on the first floor, but the upper storeys again teem with sculptural detail between tall windows. It is Secessionist in spirit, wonderfully uninhibited in scrollwork. Emerging onto Ulitsa Bratya Miladinovi (the brothers were Macedonian freedom-fighters and writers), I found an extraordinary flowering of Egyptian-style columns on a late fin-de-siècle house dated 1909. The 1911 house on the corner, as usual opulent with stucco, caught the eye with bunches of red peppers hanging above a first-floor balcony above the sign 'Hranitelni Stoki' which English translates only imperfectly into 'Foodstuffs'. Number 30 (also around 1911) is distinguished by balcony-supports fronted by lions' heads.

Bulevard Hristo Botev bustles with characters shaped by personal and national upheavals: one might guess that that gnarled man, his back bent almost horizontal, suffered industrial accidents or worse. Margarita and I chatted to a lady in her sixties, wrinkled beyond her years by frustration. 'I

Union of Stonemasons, Bul. Hristo Botev

bought my apartment up there,' she confided, 'from the Government after the seizures of '48, but now I'm terrified of what will happen if the previous owners come to claim it back, as the new law will enable them to do.' At no. 71 a bookshop occupies the corner of 3 April and Botev. Next door a noble mansion in Secessionist style (1924) belonged to the Union of Stonemasons, an honoured guild. It seemed neglected, so we went through the passageway and into the courtyard, filled appropriately with masonry fragments and lesser garbage, and there we found a charming 19th-century home of modest dimensions with a plain wooden balcony of the type you will find across the Balkan Range, sheltering the residents from rain in winter and sun in summer: an extraordinary vision in Sofia of the 1990s, like finding Anne Hathaway's cottage off Grosvenor Square.

Botev 70 needs urgent restoration to its exterior, when it would revive like a lawn after showers. It is the Kolchakov-Zafirov mansion, with commercial property downstairs as usual, and superb accommodation above it, alas wrecked by subdivision. The second floor – taken as a whole – possesses balconies on three sides, a terrace beyond a winter-garden, two bathrooms and a utilities-room, a kitchen, four rooms, and a spacious period salon hardly altered since 1912. We were invited to look around apartment 15 by Vaskresi and Nevena Zaharievi.

'Before the Law concerning Private Property was passed, the building belonged to a bankrupt company, so it reverted to the bank, which was owned by the Government. The Government then sold it to us, so we have no problems about former owners coming to claim it. There were originally three families in this apartment, but now it is divided into only two. We paid 7,500 leva for 100 square metres; now one square metre costs between 2,000 and 4,000 leva so the space we occupy would cost us these days around 300,000 leva.'

Nevena explained that she and her parents own a house built around 1939-42 in the centre of Sliven. Because her father owned a small sock factory which was expropriated by the Government in 1948, they were thrown out of the two storeys above the factory where they were living and found themselves penniless on the streets with three children to support. It is now a post office, and Nevena hopes under the new law to reclaim it for her family. But if it had been allocated to a family like her own, how could she both obtain justice and prevent innocent people being thrown out into the street again?

The land reform law has created more problems than it has solved. How do you recover land which a factory was built on?

Or farmland where a house or ten houses have been erected? Tenure is now seemingly awarded to an occupier of a house built on land owned by someone else, or to the land-owner if he had built the house. Equally, if you reclaim land that was once yours, you have to produce on it or it will revert to the previous farmer. No matter what the complexities, it has to be done, and there has never been a system equally fair to all. Better to help those disadvantaged by the former regime to spread the unfairness more evenly.

15: THEATRES

I ran, late because of a waitress's extraordinary delay, to the Ivan Vazov National Theatre for a stunning performance of Molière's *Don Juan,* played to a 30% capacity audience with Stefan Danaïlov in the leading part. The proscenium arch stage is traditional, and this is the showpiece for the best classical drama in the capital. Nothing but the neo-classical exterior of 1904 by the Viennese architects Felmer and Helmer survived the fire of 1923; in its present form the theatre dates from 1929, to the design of the German architect Dülfer. Acting styles and costumes, sets and poise: all except the language combined to evoke Molière's vision of Spain through cynical 18th-century French eyes, and nobody should miss a chance – anywhere – to see contemporary Bulgarian acting. The interval also made a dramatic impact, excited teenagers sipping Schweppes Bitter Lemon and munching Borovets chocolate wafers from the buffet, while serious citizens queued quietly for cigarettes, chocolate, and open salami sandwiches. The repertory on the main stage at the National Theatre included Tennessee Williams' *Cat on a Hot Tin Roof,* Maeterlinck's *Blue Bird, Hamlet*, Ibsen's *Peer Gynt,* and plays by Radichkov, Kovačević, Vezhinov, Haitov, Minkov, Vazov, Shatrov and Tsanev. The smaller stage offered pieces by Peter Shaffer, James Saunders, Dudarev, Strashimirov, Anastasov and Galin.

If you arrive early for a show on a summer evening, sit down beside the pool and watch the passers-by. There strides a purposeful civil servant, with a slim brown document-case, decorous in a matching suit. Yonder two shy teenagers are courting with the earnestness of those who have paddled, but never swum. Over there a woman of forty in a dark grey dress and a navy handbag stands with her feet apart the prescribed distance, balancing her glance between absorption and absentmindedness. A war veteran on the theatre steps delves deep into a newspaper's words for double meanings, triple insinuations. A flighty girl in a yellow dress trips ostentatiously beside the pool so that Heaven is allowed to glimpse her legs in the reflection.

I thought in my ignorance that the National Army Theatre at 98 Ul. Rakovski would devote its persistent labours to strident battle scenes of men in uniform shooting each other and writhing on the floor in exactly the best sightlines. But the Cold War thawed out, and interspersed with plays by Stanislav Stratiev and Konstantin Iliev the theatre puts on Beckett's *Waiting for Godot,* and especially Brecht's *Herr Puntila und sein Knecht Matti* with such pungent pugilistic gusto and wit that I wondered how much the director owed to the authentic tradition of the Berliner Ensemble. Brecht's *Entfremdungseffekt* drapes naturally on Bulgarian actors' shoulders, and this is by any standard an epoch-making production.

The Drama Theatre repertory on Bulevard Zaimov during one stay in Sofia included Erdman's controversial *The Suicide,* Georg Büchner's *Woyzeck,* and works by Valeri Petrov and I. Radoev. The Youth Theatre at 10 Ul. Narodno Subranie offered Friedrich Dürrenmatt's *King John,* a version of *Alice in Wonderland,* and works by Cocteau and Dario Fo.

The playgoing public of Sofia has been treated in recent months to a plethora of absurdism, from Eugène Ionesco's *La Cantatrice Chauve* to Harold Pinter's *The Homecoming* and Samuel Beckett's *Happy Days.*

How appropriate that the little paradoxes and huge absurdities in life after Communism, while Communists are still buzzing around calling themselves Socialists, should be reflected in the evening's entertainment. The news is straight-faced as always, but jokes proliferate, and the well-tried patience of the Sofiote is pushed to breaking-point.

If it still exists, check the weekly magazine *Edna Sedmitsa v Sofia (One Week in Sofia)* which is on sale at some kiosks, or look for posters stuck around city walls. Some performances may be on at the National Palace of Culture, or at Teatur 199, 8 Ulitsa Slavianska; the Aleko Konstantinov State Satirical Theatre at 26 Ulitsa Stefan Karaja; and the Academic Theatre of the Sarafov Higher Drama School, 108 Ulitsa Rakovski. High standards are maintained at the Central Puppet Theatre at 14 Ulitsa Gurko.

Most performances of theatre, music, opera and ballet begin at 7, and assume you will dine afterwards.

Concerts of classical music are held at the Bulgaria Concert Hall (between Rakovski and the Sofia City Garden, close to the National Theatre), and at the National Palace of Culture, now called Sofia Congress Centre.

One of the most inspiring evenings at a theatre I have ever experienced came at the House of the Lawyers in September 1991, at the eightieth-anniversary production of Peyo Yavorov's play set in 1910 *V polit' na Vitosha,* which could be translated 'On the Slopes of Vitosha'. As usual, great performances can be acted in any language with little diminution of the purely dramatic impact, and here magnificent performances shone throughout the cast, from the intense young Mariana Zhikich as Mila and Petur Burbanov as Stefan to the haunted Veselin Kalanovski as Hristo and the vibrant Madeleine Cholakova as Elizaveta.

After the show I talked to Petur Budevsky, the director, whose grandmother had created the rôle of Mila at the National Theatre in 1911. He spoke of the need to cut the original play from its five-hour length to suit a restive modern audience, about the difficulty of assembling the set for 450 leva, or about US$30, and of persuading the actors to give their services for a notional percentage of the profits. The composer and musician was played by Tsenko Minkin, whose astonishing likeness to Yavorov caused a buzz of murmurs in the excited audience.

It's difficult for westerners to appreciate the wonder generated by such productions by the newly-formed Svoboden Tea-

Svoboden Teatur. The cast of Yavorov's On the Slopes of Vitosha (House of Lawyers, Ul. 3 April)

tur ('Free Theatre'), but the high-spirited party in the house restaurant after the show indicated how well the actors thought everything had gone. It could have been a private show for a wealthy merchant and his friends, with authentic costumes, and a pocket-size hall filled with friends and acquaintances.

'Actually', confessed Petur, 'nobody can run a theatre like this in the present financial crisis without outside help. Take me: my father is a distinguished urologist and he helps to keep my family alive. I earn a living by running the state-subsidised theatre in the Palace of Culture in Pernik, an industrial city to which the actors and myself commute from Sofia most days. I'm now rehearsing Carlo Collodi's children's play *Pinocchio* because that is what the management want, but you can just picture my frustration ...'

All the actors sat with me around a table in the restaurant, drinking mainly beer and Cola, except for Mariana, who made a swift departure like an angel on wings, after shaking my hand and blushing. 'She's our great hope for the future,' murmured Veselin, 'but she's still at drama school.'

Madeleine, a vivacious star of intelligence and sophistication, spoke of her years under the Communist yoke. 'I graduated from the Drama Academy in 1977, and from then on I had to play a constant stream of proletarian women without a thought in their heads and without a personality of their own, in drab clothes to match our proletarian ideology. CAN YOU IMAGINE what I had to do through?' Her eyes sparkled with wrathful defiance, a *grande dame manquée*. She, another Sarah Bernhardt, born for Phèdre or Antigone! 'When I wasn't a socialist shock worker in a film, I was an ardent socialist handmaiden to a revolutionary on the stage. Me, in a textile factory! My favourite part was Laura in Tennessee Williams' *A Glass Menagerie*: there was a chance to express a part of my character with psychological penetration. Of all the parts I haven't played, Shaw's St Joan would be my ideal. But of course the theatre in Bulgaria is collapsing for lack of support: unlike opera singers, we actresses can't go to Italy or Austria. My family couldn't survive without the generosity of my father in New York'.

She, Veselin, and a number of other dedicated anti-Communists, had created the Free Theatre in Sofia as an antidote to the socialist realism still entrenched in state drama. Madeleine wrote her motto in capital letters to head my notes: 'If dogs run free, why don't we?'

The club lights were extinguished at 11 p.m., so they all embraced me, shook hands, and bade farewell from their different directions, never to meet me again.

16: KLIMENT OHRIDSKI UNIVERSITY

A major landmark, and junction of bus and tramlines, is the University named for the scholar Kliment of Ohrid. Funds were presented by the two brothers whose dark, seated statues survey the traffic not far from Eagles' Bridge and make a clearly definable meeting-point. I often say to those coming to meet me from a distant quarter of the capital: 'I'll meet you by Evlogi Georgiev', who sits in perpetuity near his brother Hristo.

Though the University dates as an institution from 1888, when four full-time and three part-time lecturers taught a Higher Course of Education to forty-three students, the design of this massive edifice began in 1906, but it was completed only in 1925-34, when its neo-Baroque façade must have looked as odd here as it does today, where Bulevard Tolbuhin meets Bulevard Ruski. The French architect collaborated with the Bulgarians Lazarov and Milanov, then Tsolov designed the university library in the northeast, and Konstantinov continued the north and south wings. The impression of academic grandeur displayed outside continues within: an oval vestibule, a great staircase, large auditoria, stained glass and expensive materials appropriate to a country where education was viewed as a lifelong process well before Unesco made it a motto.

Sofia University currently teaches more than forty subjects in fourteen faculties, with twenty thousand students being taught by 11 academicians, 135 professors, 340 readers and 760 assistant professors. 'Students' can be of any age, and if you want to meet them, just go downstairs into the 'Egg' as their café is known, and sit down. The chances are that you will be shyly approached by a group of students who want to know where you come from and what you think of Bulgaria:

Shivarov's monument to Evlogi Georgiev, joint founder of Sofia University

in English if you like, or possibly in French, Russian, German, Spanish or Italian. Students are naturally inquisitive, and will be glad to reciprocate your interest in them.

Because the established universities are to a very great extent influenced by attitudes and policies of the past, and Sofia University not least, new universities and colleges are springing up across the country, and in Sofia the New Bulgarian University on Bulevard Levski is already functioning with some zest, erratically, with some departments much stronger than others, but with a definite twinkle in its eye...

Just as the ordinary folk feel very suspicious of the former government's attitudes, policies and practices being transposed into the new government, so the students of N.B.U. fear that their supposedly democratic new education may be hijacked by the new dogmas of anti-Communism and hectic laissez-faire materialism. After all, the Democratic Party has already openly attacked the N.B.U. for not following the Democratic Party-political line. In a country where freedom of speech and breadth of sympathy have always been suspect, it will take decades for a real education based on the open mind to emerge from old prejudice.

17: THE NATIONAL ART GALLERY AND ETHNOGRAPHIC MUSEUM

The Ottoman Konak, where the Sultan's district representative or *beylerbey* resided, passed on Liberation in 1878 to Prince Alexander Battenberg, for whom it was reconstructed in 1883-1890. King Ferdinand then occupied it, expanding and modernising the Bulgarian Renaissance building in the Viennese Baroque style favoured by Grunänger and it became a charming, unassuming residence of Boris III, and then after his death in 1943 of his widow. Taken over by the Council of Ministers after the royal family had been exiled, in 1954 it was opened as the national art gallery in the west wing, and the national ethnographic museum, in the east wing.

How does a European art tradition survive five centuries of Islamic prohibitions? Representational artists in other cultures subjected to Quranic domination, the Turks and the Greeks, the Iraqis and the Egyptians, have found their own ways of counteracting doctrinal intransigence; in Bulgaria resistance begins with the National Revival, first with Zahari Zograf of Samokov (1810-53) and the friend of Garibaldi, Dimitur Dobrovich (1816-1905). Their self-portraits throw down the gauntlet to fundamentalists who would forbid human figures, as does that of Nikolai Pavlovich (1835-94), who founded the Bulgarian Academy of Fine Arts. Portraiture develops with Hristo Tsokev's 'Angelina Bruchkova' (1874) and his wife (1875). Zahari's nephew Stanislav Dospevski also concentrated on portraits: here are his father Dimitur, Smaragda Samokovleva, and Ekaterina Hajigyurova. (In Bulgaria the prefix Haji indicates that one has made the Orthodox pilgrimage to Jerusalem.) The murals of Sofia's Sveta Nedelya are recalled by seeing Dospevski's intriguing work. Some icons and murals in the Nevski Cathedral are by Anton Mitov (1862-1930), whose self-portrait understandably conceals more than it states: a suggestion of half-held beliefs, the propagation of half-truths insisting on compromise as a basic human need.

The Czech Jan Mrkvička (1856-1938) worked so long in Bulgaria that he is claimed as a native son, as El Greco is claimed by Spain. His famous 'Rachenitsa' depicts an endurance dance in a village pub, but the subtler 'Virgin' creates a deeper resonance. The first significant woman artist in Bulgaria, Elena Karamihailova, is represented by a portrait of her sister. Nikola Petrov (1881-1916) has a view of the Rhodope village Chepino, and his 'Orlov Most' (Eagles' Bridge) of 1910 shows Sofia's trams nine years after their introduction.

Horizons widened when Bulgarian artists began to study and travel abroad after Liberation in 1878, but the vast majority of their landscapes refer back to their homeland and people. Stefan Ivanov (1875-1951) portrays the beloved poetess Dora Gabe; Hristo Stanchev (1870-1950) stirs our imagination with 'In the Field' and Atanas Mihov (1879-1950) recalls those days when there were still 'Icebergs on the Danube'. The plastically monumental painter of pre-Communist times, Ivan Nenov, born in 1902, has delightful portraits of women and girls of the 1930s. Zlatyu Boyajiev, cruelly paralysed at 40, is represented by a vibrant 'Winter in Plovdiv' near Tsanko Lavrenov's 'Old Plovdiv'. I dislike the overblown rhetoric of Vladimir Dimitrov (1882-1960), but sympathise with the more sensitive portraits by Dechko Uzunov: 'The Actor Sarafov' (1932) and 'Myself at 84' (1983).

The two other departments of the gallery are devoted to socialist realism after 1944, and a range of foreign artists, from Italy, the Low Countries, France and Russia.

The National Ethnographic Museum is particularly rich, despite the destruction of many items during World War II air-raids by the Allies. Recent additions have brought the collections to a total of 70,000, of which very few can be shown. Most towns in Bulgaria have their own ethnographic museums, so if your time in Sofia is limited and you plan to visit provincial cities, it might be preferable to concentrate on unique objects in the National History Museum rather than works you can find duplicated elsewhere, such as embroidery and costume, objects of wood, copper and gold, leather, wrought iron and pottery. The vast majority of Bulgarians have always lived on the land, and practised farming or fishing, stockbreeding and handicrafts. Rituals and festivals have played a great part in the lives of country folk: look for musical instruments such as the *gaida* and mummers' masks from pagan *kukeri* rites still practised today.

Across from the Royal Palace is the contrasting plain white mausoleum of Georgi Dimitrov, patron saint of Bulgarian Communism, whose reputation in Sofia was akin to that of Lenin in Moscow. Dimitrov (1882-1949) and his close friend and colleague Vasil Kolarov (buried nearby) had lived and worked as political commissars in the Soviet Union until they

Ploshtad Battenberg, with Royal Palace (now National Art Gallery, left) and Dimitrov Mausoleum (1949, right)

felt the time was ripe to come back and take control in 1945 under the growing power of the Fatherland Front. Peasant suspicions of Soviet-style collective farming led to a new solution in Bulgaria. Here, membership of cooperatives was voluntary and those who chose to join did not have to surrender all their land for privileges. They received a ground rent for land they chose to surrender, but many still preferred their old Agrarian Party to the alien doctrine of Communism introduced from Russia. In 1944 the fur, coal and rubber industries had been nationalised and other industries followed, including alcohol and soft drinks. Impoverishment of the bourgeoisie and private concerns was completed by various economic and fiscal measures, with ruinous tax bands, and seizure of assets. After Dimitrov had made Nikola Petkov a scapegoat, he cynically dissolved Petkov's Agrarian Party as 'a centre for fascist forces seeking revenge' though it was no more fascist than he was. By 1948, the Fatherland Front had acquired all the previously independent social and trade union organisations except one or two such as the Social Democrats headed by Kosta Lulchev. The party was disbanded in 1948 and Lulchev condemned to fifteen years in jail as a traitor, for voting against the Communists' budget. Dimitrov died in Moscow in July 1949 and was succeeded by the elderly Kolarov, who died six months later.

Dimitrov's mausoleum, the only non-Soviet leader's in the Communist world, has been disfigured since the anti-Communist coup of November 1989. Graffiti of all types have been daubed in black and red across the white surfaces. Slogans of the Union of Democratic Forces, exhortations to monarchist fervour, even a swastika. Nobody washes them off, knowing full well that they would be rewritten, ever more savagely, by descendants of those who lost their life or liberty in the prolonged struggle against Communism. Across the top, someone has sprayed in Bulgarian 'The Biggest Shithouse in Europe'.

Such deeply offensive and crude graffiti, seeming to run counter to Bulgaria's age-old reputation for courtesy, indicate the divisions that Dimitrov and his successors as presidents of Communist Bulgaria caused throughout the country. A member of the Parliament from 1913 to 1923, Dimitrov was forced into exile into the Soviet Union when his coup against the Government failed. He came to world prominence in September 1933 when he faced Goering in Leipzig at the Reichstag fire trial in September 1933, a trial documented in a film called *The Warning*. Released from prison when the U.S.S.R. granted him Soviet citizenship, he was appointed Secretary of the Communist International, or Comintern. In September 1935 he sent out a call for world solidarity of the proletariat, urging workers to curb the rise of Fascism.

And what happened to his embalmed body? After the first free post-war elections, held in 1990, the Government decided to remove Dimitrov's body from the mausoleum and to follow his own dying wishes: that he should be cremated and his ashes laid in the same grave as his mother, in the Central Sofia Cemetery. It is there that one should call if one wishes to pay respects to the memory of the first post-war President of Bulgaria.

18: AN EVENING WITH THE MONARCHISTS

All over Sofia the posters announced a Concert-Spectacle sponsored jointly by the Bulgarian Union for European Federation, the Royal Automobile Club and the Conservative Party to be held at Sofia Opera House on 13 September 1991 to mark the 45th anniversary of the exile from the fatherland of His Royal Highness Simeon II, King of the Bulgarians and the royal family.

Would this be a chance for the Socialists to wave banners in a contra-march? Would the monarchists rant and rave? No, of course not. Mass rallies by the U.D.F. one evening and the B.S.P. the next at the same venue, in front of the Royal

Monarchists at a democratic rally (September 1991)

Palace and the Dimitrov Mausoleum had passed without clashes, so a celebration of regal pomp and nostalgia was hardly likely to be frustrated. And so it turned out, for I attended both political rallies before the October 1991 elections, and the evening with the monarchists.

Beneath glittering chandeliers the well-dressed audience buzzed with expectation, for such a gathering, such an event, occurred rarely even in post-Zhivkov times. I sat next to the chic Jeanne Drenikova, a repetiteuse at the opera, aunt of the soprano Valerie Popova, and great-aunt of the gifted young guest Gilda of Welsh National Opera, Alexandrina Pendachanska. Before curtain up, the evening's audience chatted gaily, or read the monarchist newspaper *Korona*. Self-conscious, well-off, and if not exactly the cream of the intelligentsia (who absent themselves from all such overt uncritical partisanship), then at least the audience belonged to the politesse, the French-speaking occidentophilic sector of society whose passionate nationalism coalesces into international royalism. They would have applauded Princess Stephanie of Monaco or Princess Diana just as effervescently. Like schoolchildren let off their daily class in Marxism-Leninism, they whispered throughout or even chattered as at an annual picnic. A picnic deferred for exactly 45 years.

A soberly-dressed compère announced to the half-incredulous assembly the reasons for their gathering, followed by a Children's Wind Band in royal uniform of red and gold. Then a dramatisation of *The Last 13 Days of Tsar Boris III* was recreated by the great actress Nevena Kokanova and the illustrious Nikolai Kalchev, based on chronicles of that period in 1943 when the monarchy suffered its last throes. Against a shimmering background of burnt sienna, golds, reds and browns a golden crown swung above the actors like an incense-burner.

In the interval, someone whispered that they had seen the desk of Prince Kiril (Boris' brother executed by the Communists) in the office of Liliana Georgieva, head of the Local Government Department of the Council of Ministers.

Which of the Sofia Opera soloists would emerge in the second half to nail their colours to the monarchist mast? Popova, due to sing Leonora's aria from *La Forza del Destino,* cried off at the last moment because she had to prepare for her daughter's departure to Pretoria tomorrow and was replaced by the glorious Daniela Nedyalkova. Rumen Doikov gave us 'La donna è mobile' from *Rigoletto,* and Stefka Mineva joined the gipsy chorus from *Trovatore* with 'Stride la vampa'. Dimitur Stanchev had come from Madrid to offer da Silva's aria from *Ernani* and the Verdian bias was completed by the Hebrew Slaves' Chorus from *Nabucco,* as rich in symbolism for monarchists after the 1989 coup as for democrats before it, and for Communists during the monarchical years. Could the wheel ever return full circle with the restoration of the Bulgarian monarchy? Who knows? Who would have given odds against it, that evening when the royal anthem and the national anthem were played one after the other by the orchestra under Boris Hinchev?

Nobody but the oldest can remember the days of the monarchy, of relative freedom and democracy. How can the younger generation create democratic institutions based on social equity, non-discrimination, fair play, and selfless work for the good of the community when all such intentions have in the past been blunted by cynicism, nepotism, discrimination, injustice, and a realisation that there would be no point in working harder for more pay (because there would be no more pay) or for a fairer society (which could not under the previous rules have come into existence)?

Communists played on fears of divisiveness, fears of the Jews, of the Muslims, of the spiritual dimensions of Christianity, so the secret police infiltrated every echelon of the body politic. They tried to persuade by bribery and corruption: when these failed they resorted to house arrest, jail, torture, and murder. A totalitarian state of mind ruled the country like a mental fog, dousing initiative, originality, eccentricity, 'the other ways'. The dangers of international communism – not only in Bulgaria but in all the other Communist states – evoked reactionary dangers of nationalistic chauvinism of the type that has destroyed the Union of Soviet Socialist Republics and Yugoslavia. The repressive nature of Ottoman Bulgaria led to the nationalistic revival of Bulgaria as a state satellite to the U.S.S.R. After World War II, nationalism was held in check by the heavy hand of Soviet orthodoxies, as they fluctuated within the kaleidoscope of Stalinism-Khrushchevism-Brezhnevism-Gorbachevism. Now perestroika has brought down Gorbachev as, for instance, the Red Army left Czechoslovakia in 1991 ahead of schedule, and simultaneously Boris Yeltsin took command in Russia.

While the exiled King Simeon II keeps his dreams alive in Madrid, who can predict the next swing of the Bulgarian pendulum?

19: ART GALLERIES

Among the best foreign art collections in Eastern Europe is the SS. Cyril and Methodius Foundation Foreign Art Gallery situated at 1 Ulitsa 19 February, on Alexander Nevski Square, in the former State Printing House designed by the Viennese architect Schwanberger at the end of the 19th century. Open since 1985, it was formerly known as the Zhivkova Foundation Gallery after the former dictator's daughter Lyudmila Zhivkova. Housing the collection donated by Kostadin Delchev, a dentist from Asenovgrad who had lived in France for more than sixty years, and his wife Claudia, it includes a fine nucleus of Christian works from Goa, six thousand prints and drawings, and fine works from Asia and Africa. More than ten thousand works in the gallery's holdings cannot be shown for lack of space: there is room for only 750, among them examples by Cornelis van Poelenburgh, van Dyck, Courbet, Rodin, Delacroix, Renoir, Maximilien Luce, Signac, Valadon, Matisse, Rouault's wrenching 'Boucher' of 1903, Villon, Vlaminck, Derain, Dunoyer de Segonzac, the Vidin-born Julius Pinkas known in Paris and his adopted New York as Jules Pascin, up to Buffet. Temporary exhibitions have been devoted to Spanish Golden Age painting, Käthe Kollwitz and Henry Moore.

I was astonished to find a Giovanni Rossi (d. 1549), son of that northern Italian Antonio Rossi known to posterity as Titian's first master who has a 'Virgin and Child' in the Venice Academy. The collection grows with donations, but problems with hard currency make it impossible to bid for major works at auction.

Bulgarian modern art is more widely available than foreign art, but only seldom rises to heights equivalent to its many French, German and Austrian influences. Sofia City Art Gallery at 1 Ulitsa Gurko (10.30-7 but closed Mondays and Tuesdays) concentrates on 20th-century works by Bulgarian artists: that is to say, those painters appearing after the Liberation. National Revival art, visible in the National Art Gallery in the Royal Palace, can also be seen here, represented by Ivan Angelov, Anton Mitov, Yaroslav Vešin and Jan Mrkvićka. We begin to see a native landscape art emerging in Vasil Barakov's 'Chepelare', a tradition developing with Naiden Petkov, Georgi Baev and Genko Genkov. It is worth exploring the halls for works by David Perez (a vivid 'Still Life' with mushrooms), Elena Karamihailova, Sirak Skitnik, the patrarchal Dechko Uzunov, Ivan Nenov, Bronka Gyurova and Svetlin Rusev, who donated a collection to the city of Pleven. Regrettably, the standard of sculpture here is rather lower. The graphic art collection is strengthened by works from Rumen Skorchev, Lyuben Dimanov and Atanas Neikov.

I much prefer the temporary exhibitions by younger artists in the Art Gallery of the Bulgarian Artists' Union at 6 Ulitsa Shipka (9-8 daily). These artists have not chosen to compromise with old and debased notions of proletarian realism, fatally wounding the spirit of innovation and imagination. The vibrant 'Profile' by Ivan Milushev of Blagoevgrad snags on my memory; amid the hasty works one is always likely to come across such a visionary poet of line and colour who feels liberated by a pluralistic community, where individualism is no longer sacrificed at the altar of collectivism. Another showroom for contemporary Bulgarian artists at 6 Bulevard Ruski is situated close to the Mineral Souvenir shop at no. 10. Other exhibition halls are to be found at 125 Rakovski, 147 Rakovski, 18a Stamboliiski and 18 Vitosha.

But the great wheel of art has begun to roll helter-skelter, and the foreigner will be invited to private studios, new galleries which spring up overnight, and pavement easels on thoroughfares. For a variety of historical reasons, craftsmen and -women have reached a level of uninhibited sophistication and originality beyond that of many artists, and if you have the chance to see applied arts in action, be sure that the prices will be well below anything you would expect to pay in Paris or New York.

20: BULEVARD RUSKI

Sofia's Russian Boulevard was named for the Tsar Liberator and his welcome hordes relieving Bulgaria from Ottoman domination, and for the Russian Church of St Nikolai (1913-4) designed by Preobrazhenski in an exuberant style which brings back memories of a stage-set for Rimsky-Korsakov's opera *Christmas Eve* perhaps, or an invigorating sleigh-ride in the city of Vladimir one dark January evening, with only waxing moon and stars for company. It was painted by the same Russian artists who had come to decorate the Nevski Cathedral: its icons, including an impressive Christ Pantocrator, are copied from those in Kiev, and its iconostasis is likewise in Russian mode. It belonged to the Russian Patriarchate until 1953, but nowadays services are in Church Slavonic, as in the rest of Bulgaria.

Ruski has a Polish Cultural Centre with a shop and exhibition, and a Hungarian Cultural Centre which to my taste provides the most original and thoughtful temporary exhibitions to be seen in Sofia: photographs, paintings, sculpture and pottery. On the other side of the Kristal Garden, artists set up temporary stalls, dealers show coins, banknotes and notes, and ladies sell their handiwork in the form of lace, crocheting and embroidery, the Czech and Slovak Shop displays and sells records, books, tapes, toys and textiles at prices higher than those of Bulgarian goods, but lower than Western figures.

The Natural History Museum at Ruski 1 was laid out to show worldwide and domestic wildlife by the Bulgarian Academy of Sciences, arranged in sequence of Darwin's theory of evolution. Opposite is the neo-classical Hotel Bulgaria, designed by the Czech architect Kolar and built in 1885-90, with a welcoming garden-restaurant unobtrusively lit at night.

The Russian Church

One morning in my Lima hotel, I heard an American at the next breakfast table say to his colleague, 'Did you hear about the bank raid near the Post Office last night?' 'Which one?', replied the other: 'I hear there were six.' Such laconic exchanges will never mar the rest of your day in Sofia, but as people become more desperate for their family's next meal, it is inevitable that thefts will occur and increase. In the city centre I generally look around for likely pickpockets, slouching youths, shifty-eyed men of indeterminate age, stubble-chinned, keen-eyed, glancing from side to side. Two of a possible gang seemed to be converging on me from opposite directions one day near the Polish Shop on Ruski. I stood stock still to watch their reactions. They stopped too, perplexed, so I slipped ostentatiously between two policemen guarding the entrance to Hotel Bulgaria and stared them out, first the black leather jacket, then the loud check shirt, then back to the leather jacket. They met for a moment, exchanged half a dozen words, and separated like a snake from its skin.

I tried to phone Iliana twice without success at two phones. The third street telephone worked, but many do not. I have never understood why the nation which gave us the Sputnik and Yuri Gagarin couldn't manage to provide a dependable water supply, a telephone system that would not die during thunderstorms, and an electricity supply that would not collapse for several hours a day. Russia was always like this, but the failure of public services and utilities spread contagiously to Romania and Bulgaria, Tajikistan and Turkmenistan. I found the shower would not work in Tashkent and Irkutsk, the power failed in Tirana and Belgrade, and the telephones gave no answer in Kiev and Dushanbe. I can see that a decentralised administration might produce uneven results, but how a mightily centralised administration with massive funds could not extend its tentacles, like a relentless octopus, into the provision of dependable public facilities: that remains inexplicable.

Ruski 3 is occupied by the concert agency, close to Zala

Bulgaria, the premier concert hall in the capital. You cannot buy tickets at the main entrance on Ulitsa Aksakov: you have to take the side turning on to Ul. Benkovski, which leads to the artists' entrance, and a small office where a lady laboriously writes out all tickets by hand, a system still operational throughout the country.

The Museum of the Revolutionary Movement at Ruski 14 was created to glorify Communist achievements at the expense of a balanced conspectus, and I am sure it will be closed ere long. If so, I hope the charming old building is repaired: it was the private house of Dr. D. Mollov, damaged by air raids, and restored on the ground floor for this propaganda museum, which identifies the course of democracy, freedom and workers' rights with the Communist Party. If you get a chance to see these displays showing one aspect of Bulgarian history from 1885 to the Zhivkov period, remember how Zhivkov's attitude to his Muslim workers in 1989 created the biggest exodus in Europe since World War II. The Communist-led Fatherland Front organised 'spontaneous' anti-Turkish demonstrations which led 350,000 people to flee in a period of ten weeks before Turkey closed its borders on 22 August. Military occupation of the Gotse Delchev tobacco-growing area until December 1989 allowed local officials to refuse the issue of passports. Villages became deserted, factories fell idle, farm animals died, houses and goods were stolen. A similar Museum of Revolutionary Vigilance at 5 Ulitsa Lavele catered for impressionable local people, but that too must be doomed in an era of political pluralism.

The Italian (1890-5) and Austrian (1900) Embassies on Ruski recall that renaissance of building in Sofia which gave us the Government Printing House of 1884, the Military School and Academy of Sciences (1892), the old Post Office (1893), the Military Club of 1895 and the Holy Synod (1904-1909). The Chinese Embassy (1906-7) at Ruski 18 was the Yablenski House, and yet another embassy on Ruski, at 27, is that of Brazil.

Ruski has no trams, except at the intersection with the en-

The Military Club (1895-1900, in a view of c. 1916)

tertainment district around Rakovski. The smooth rectangular yellow tiles become so diabolically shiny and slippery under winter ice that an incautious run can cause you to break a leg, or a car to skid and kill you. Take care.

21: LITERARY MUSEUMS

Just as literary pilgrims to Italy head for Dante Alighieri's
Fiesole and Ravenna, and pilgrims to England make first for
Shakespeare's Stratford-upon-Avon, so those visiting Bulgaria should allow time for the House-Museum of the national
poet Ivan Vazov (1850-1921), at 10 Ul. Vazov, open at eccen-
tric hours but certainly closed from Saturday afternoon till
Tuesday noon. Photographs, books, quotations and documents try to evoke the spirit of a man of letters and action:
here he is at Kalofer (1865-6), at Sopot (1870), at Berkovitsa
(1879-80), at Odessa in 1888 (he lived by coincidence at Sofia
St. there, later no. 32 Korolenko St.). A bedroom with a single
bed and simple washstand is made claustrophobic by heavy
muffling curtains and a tall glazed stove like a solid intruder
forever looking over your shoulder to check you are hard at
work. Thick drapes seem to half-fill the silent private library,
with Vazov's sofa, rocking-chair, early telephone and that
'desk' for which he retained such affection, though it is no
more than a plain deal table topped with baize. His friends
urged him to buy a more 'suitable' desk: one of the legs was
shorter than the rest and needed to be propped up with wads
of paper. 'No', replied Vazov, 'what matters is *what* a man
writes, not the piece of furniture *where* he writes'. The best
painting here is *Macedonia* by the Czech-born painter Jan
Mrkvička. The bookshelves are lined with Victor Hugo and
Schiller, Zola and Shakespeare, as well as editions of his own
works, such as *Pod Igoto* ('Under the Yoke'). Wallpaper
printed red on cream, another stove and more heavy drapes
clutter the sitting-room. His mother's bedroom's walls are
decked with sepia photos, as is the dining-room, back downstairs, where he died. The birch is surrounded, in the little
garden, by sad cypress. Vazov's house foundations were laid

103

in March 1895 and by that September he, his brother Nikola and his mother had moved in, next door to the family of his younger sister Vula. The house was destroyed by an incendiary bomb on 30 March 1944, and reopened in its present form in 1950.

A nation's soul is not visible: it resides in the poetry, plays and great novels of its writers, so while on my way to the 'Sulza i Smyah' ('Tears and Laughter') Theatre at 127 Ul. Rakovski I wanted to find time to breathe in the atmosphere of two more museum-houses: Peyo Yavorov's at 136 Ul. Rakovski and Petko and Pencho Slaveikov's next door at 138. Like the other literary houses once inhabited by Hristo Smirnenski (116 Ul. Shekerjiiski) and by Nikola Vaptsarov (37 Ul. Kanchev), the opening-times are 12-7 on Tuesdays and Wednesdays, 9-5 on Thursdays and Fridays, and 9-1 on Saturdays. Yavorov (1878-1914) a prominent poet and playwright, spent the last years of his wife Laura's life here, in a late 19th-century house, before she committed suicide in a fit of jealous torment. Born Kracholov, Peyo withdrew into himself after losing faith in socialism and the possibilities of the proletariat, and having struggled for Macedonia, though not a Macedonian himself. Here is the map of Macedonia he himself used, 1899-1903, with pistols and rifles. His study broods with the burden of self-murder like an indelible shadow. Laura, daughter of the party leader Petko Karavelov, had committed suicide earlier. 'I'm coming after you', he wrote but merely lost his sight: the second time he shot himself he also took poison to make doubly sure. The desk, bookshelves, candlesticks breathe the name of a man imbued with Russian symbolism, French symbolism, who could entitle a 1907 volume of poems *Insomnia and Intuitions* and penned dramas in the penumbra of Chekhov such as *At the Foot of Mount Vitosha* (1911) and *When the Thunder Rolls* (1912). The guest-room where literary friends came to visit is opposite the original bedroom of Laura and Peyo. Here are souvenirs of Peyo's mistress Mina Todorova, his muse while they lived in France for a full year, who inspired his best love poems, such as 'Two

Beautiful Eyes'. Furniture from the sitting-room opposite the study comes from the house Yavorov lived in after Laura's death.

Bulgaria's great intellectual and poet Petko Slaveikov was born in 1827 the son of Racho Kazanjiyata of Veliko Turnovo. Though Racho was a domineering personality, Petko rebuked him with words which have resounded down the decades since then: 'Na zhivot mi si gospoda, no na volyata ne mi si', a melodious aphorism that might be translated 'You are the master of my life, but not of my will'. In 1879 Petko and his son Pencho came to Sofia and their lives here are illustrated in a room left of the entrance. Pencho collaborated with Yavorov in publishing collections of Bulgarian folksongs, and translated German poets in addition to *Romeo and Juliet* and *The Taming of the Shrew*. The original house on the site was destroyed, but many of its contents survived, and other memorabilia have been added. Here is Petko's library, quill pen, snuff-box, a watch showing European and Bulgarian time, neatly exemplifying the distance separating Sofia from the vortex of European life. In Pencho's room I pored over photos of his father and his sister Penka, and the residue of his once excellent library: some two thousand books in nine languages: Euripides, Goethe, Heine, Nietzsche, Verlaine. Another room is devoted to Pencho's companion Marya Belcheva, widow of a Minister of Finance during the Stamboliiski government who was assassinated when Marya was only 23. A confidante of Ferdinand's mother, Clementine, Marya lived with Pencho from the age of 35 to the end of his life, closing his eyes at Brunate on Lake Como in 1912, when he was 46. Her room displays a glass lamp from Venice: how fragile is life compared with glass!

Slaveikov rejected Vazov's realism, seizing as models the balladic spirit of German literature, and Nietzsche's passionate invocation of human possibilities in an age ruled by religion and obscurantism. He transcended national boundaries in clarity of Russian tragic intensity. Never wholly emerging from his father's giant shadow (one thinks of Witkiewicz in

Poland and his son Witkacy; or Gosse's sado-masochistic *Father and Son*), Pencho nevertheless worked out his destiny in part during the Leipzig years (1892-8), in flashes of originality in his nature poetry, and above all in the magazine *Misul* ('Thought') produced jointly for seventeen years with Yavorov, Krustev, and Todorov.

22: TEA WITH THE COLONEL

Grigor's mystery tour by bus brought us to Lyulin, a waste zone of multi-storey apartments, each containing its own drama, northwest of Sofia.

The socialist architects who designed these ghastly high-rise apartment blocks were not allowed the space or the money to landscape these districts, so that for fresh air and recreation people have to take a tram to the Freedom Park or Vitosha instead of being able to stroll in neighbourhood gardens with allotments to grow fruit and vegetables. As always, these districts which 'belonged to the people' in fact belonged to nobody in particular, and so were never cherished. The result is that no lawns or trees survive, and litter is trodden into winter slush or borne listlessly about by autumn winds.

'Meet my cousin the Colonel', he said, as the lift jolted to a standstill on the nth floor. 'Colonel as in the Army?'

A sharply raucous ring on the doorbell fetched a nervous lady in apron and slippers.

'Panka,' smiled Grigor. 'Just wait', she said.

Grigor explained that she was hurriedly tidying up so that I should find her home in apple-pie order. At a given word a portly man with a red face and hastily-donned trousers emerged from the kitchen with arms outstretched.

'Stefcho!'

They embraced briefly as cousins will, and I shook hands with the Colonel before proffering vodka. We sat down around the kitchen table as family, while Panka produced a pot of tea and Stefan busied himself with glasses and a bottle of rakia. Panka then found a tray of biscuits and Stefan sliced open a fresh water-melon.

The window stood open to allow the August heat to disperse: a laconic breath of air occasionally deigned to float

Lyulin. A block of apartments

around our heads, but generally the atmosphere remained stiff with desert drought. The ripe, cool water-melon sank into my mouth and throat like rain into an oasis.

After courtesies, I suggested it would have been unthinkable a few months back for a Bulgarian army colonel to invite a foreigner to his flat. He spread his arms wide to encompass the room. 'Now we are friends with the whole world', he agreed in Bulgarian, 'but before we are like horses with blinkers, going down only one road and not allowed to see the intersections, the highways, the alleys, the parallel roads.' He apologised for speaking only Bulgarian and Russian. 'These were the army languages before, now I must learn English because it's the language of NATO. But all these ideas are very new, and I don't know how we older officers will cope.'

'How do you see the alliances changing?'

'I hope that all the former Soviet republics will form one unified peaceful confederation, with a single defence policy and a unified nuclear arsenal.'

'Do you think that the army will move from conscription to professionalism?'

'It must be, but we hear it will take minimal five years. We have to encourage dedication, but the reason this is difficult is because we have to move away from the politicisation of the past to a depoliticised future. You can't have a Communist army in a democratic republic, or vice versa. We shall always need an army. Our only peaceful neighbour is Greece. Romania will always be volatile because of the Latin temperament of the people. Yugoslavia will always be unstable, because Tito threw together a bundle of squawking cats in a bag, and they will always scratch each other's eyes out. Obviously Turkey will always be a potential danger, because of the kind of territorial ambitions we have seen in the occupation of Northern Cyprus. They think that part of Southern Bulgaria belongs to them. Despite the turning back of the Ottoman swarms at the liberation of Bulgaria, Turks will always look longingly at Bulgaria.'

We finished our rakia. Grigor said to Panka, 'What hap-

109

pened to your cat?'

Everywhere I am upset by the sight of cats and kittens, thin and mangy, underfed and underloved, as scared as the toms in Thurber cartoons. They seem neglected in a country where all food is expensive, yet prodigally offered to guests, where finding enough food even for your family is a major exercise in planning, queuing and the diplomacy of exchange.

Panka replied, 'I had to have it put down. We couldn't afford food both for the child and for the cat.'

Outside the oppressive kitchen, a plane droned on and on, encircling Vitosha.

23: CINEMA

Lenin's famous dictum that cinema is the most important of the arts concealed the prescription that film-producers should be even more responsive than all other producers of mass culture to the needs of socialist propaganda. 'Art for art's sake' was never a Communist slogan and if you wanted to assert the artist's necessary individualism (Leonardo, Mozart, Picasso, James Joyce) you had to leave the proletarian paradise of Eastern Europe, or remain isolated, forgotten, poor and unrecognised.

For the individualistic stay-at-home film director, reliant on state facilities and state-trained actors, there could be no such escape. For him, the alternative to conformity lay in silence.

That is why I was particularly stimulated by recent Bulgarian films such as Rangel Vulchanov's *A Sega na Kude?* ('Where do we go from here?') for a bunch of rebellious young actors, and the James Dean-ish *Margarit i Margarita* (Margarit is a masculine name in Bulgarian) by Nikolai Volev which I saw at the Levski Cinema near the tennis courts at 28 Bulevard Zaimov. The price of a ticket is 3 leva at present, or less than 25 US cents. Shows begin at 10, then either 2, 4, 6 and 8 p.m. or 1, 3, 5, 7 and 9 p.m. A great many American films reach Sofia these days, and some are dubbed, but most are subtitled. Some cinemas, such as the Serdika on Vasil Levski Square, pin up a list of films showing at other cinemas to enable you to choose on the spot, and some of the proliferation of daily newspapers print the same or fuller information, if you can read Cyrillic. For archive films, the best cinema is Druzhba at 1 Patriarch Eftimii. Modern films shown at other cinemas often appeal to the lower end of the spectrum. These include the Dimitur Blagoev (no. 35) and the

111

Moskva (no. 52) on Ulitsa Alabin, the Globus at 2 Ul. Solunska, the Slaveikov on Slaveikov Square, the Kultura at 11 Ul. Graf Ignatiev, and the Macedonia on 5 Ul. 3 April.

Vulchanov and Volev demanded attention from the whole of society. *Margarit i Margarita* pits the emerging younger generation against a corrupt and wicked older generation that defends its excesses when challenged. It also specifically accuses a Party boss of abusing his position to obtain sexual favours. Georgi Dyulgerov's *The Camp* dares to address issues of injustice and brutality inherent in every kind of totalitarian dictatorship. Lyudmil Todorov's *The Last Summer of a Schlepp* portrays doomed innocence, as four students enjoy leisure on Black Sea beaches before beginning the dreary lives they recognise lie before them in the world of work and conformist society. Docho Bujakov's *Who Art in Heaven* contrasts what he perceives as dour and monotonous Bulgarian society with the high culture of Central Europe, revealing his distaste for the former and his envy of an open society, liberated intellectuals, the freedom to travel, and tolerance of other people's values and morals. In *I, the Countess,* Petur Popzlatev daringly proposes that drug addiction can be a method for the young to reject the doctrinaire state and its narrow expectations: it is a film that points the way to a pluralist film industry – to the full acceptance of Bulgaria within the highly idiosyncratic artistic West during the last decade of the century.

That is not to say that the 300-acre Boyana Studios complex had not ever made controversial movies in its thirty years of existence; but satirical and 'truthful' movies were simply withheld from general release. In June 1991 the Bulgarian Cinematography State Corporation was closed down and replaced by a National Film Board on Canadian lines, which will register independent producers, subsidise them up to about 80% of their costs, and expect them to find the balance from private sources. The Board will classify films as artistic, commercial or pornographic and tax them accordingly, artistic films rating the lowest tax. Censorship now exists to prohibit military and anti-religious films, and in terms of age to classify productions as generally suitable, only for 16 and over, and 18 and over. There is a large reservoir of trained technicians, actors and directors, many available for hire by foreign film producers who will also be able to lease the Boyana Studios in the expected absence of much new production by domestic producers.

24: ALEXANDER NEVSKI MEMORIAL CATHEDRAL AND RELIGIOUS MUSEUMS

Over the years, I have come to appreciate the great affection that Sofiotes feel for the monumental complex of Ploshtad Narodno Subranie (National Assembly Square), in which the neo-classical National Assembly (1884-1928) faces the Tsar Liberator, Alexander II, waving his declaration of war against Turkey above Russian troops, with bronze groups around his pedestal commemorating the Battle for Stara Zagora (1877), the Treaty of San Stefano (1878) and the Assembly of Turnovo (1879). The sculptor is the Italian Arnaldo Zocchi (1862-1940), whose Garibaldi monument is not my favourite sculpture in Bologna. On one side of the square stands the enormous Grand Hotel Sofia (1969), on another side the main building of the Bulgarian Academy of Sciences, whose branches dot the city. But the square is overtopped by the great green and golden domes of the Memorial Cathedral named for Alexander Nevski, erected between 1904 and 1912 and consecrated in 1924. It pays tribute to the Russian dead as well as to the Bulgarian dead who fought and lost their lives during the struggle for liberation from Ottoman control. The 13th-century Prince of Novgorod was Tsar Alexander II's patron saint because he saved Russia from invading Swedish armies in 1240.

Interestingly, the modern cathedral overlies a part of Serdica's millennial necropolis, at the modern capital's highest level. You can see a part of this necropolis near Hagia Sophia.

Matters of status and precedence have been dealt with as tactfully as traditional iconography will allow. Thus, while the central iconostasis is Russian, those lateral to it are Bulgarian (on the south, the patron saint being King Boris I) and Slavic (on the north, the patron saints being Cyril and Meth-

Parliament Square, with the Bulgarian Academy of Sciences (left), the National Assembly (right), and St Alexander Nevski

odius). Thirty-two Russian artists worked on the frescoes in the centre and thirteen Bulgarian artists under Anton Mitov painted elsewhere. Ferdinand never sat on the throne he ordered: it was used by Boris III. The Bishop's throne behind formed part of Pomerantsev's original plan. Subjects of the murals include 'Christ in the Temple' (grids in the wall have been ingeniously incorporated as seats into the pattern) painted in 1924; Boris I, who converted to Christianity in 865; and Vladimir, who introduced it to Russia in 980. It is not fair to comment adversely on the artistic standard of Kisselev's 'Nativity of Christ', 'Baptism' or 'Last Judgment' because these works had to be compatible with a building intended to bolster national fervour rather than continue the mainstream of religious painting which has evolved elsewhere through Chagall, let us say, or Stanley Spencer in their own individualistic ways. Bulgaria's profound isolation from modernism in art paralleled that of Russia, for much the same obvious historical reasons, and we must accept Nevski Cathedral for what it is, not regret what it might have been.

Alexander Nevski has absorbed new-Byzantine, Russian, and even Romanesque styles in its new unity. A functioning church, it pays tribute like Shipka Memorial Church (1897-1902) to the two hundred thousand Russians who fell while achieving Bulgaria's liberation in 1877-8. Its great choir, specialising in liturgical music, has made first-rate but very cheap gramophone records and cassettes normally on sale from the ladies selling candles who occupy booths within the narthex. Of the twelve bells, the smallest weigh 10 kg and the largest 12 tons: this latter tolls on Sunday mornings, and to attend a Sunday service is to participate in the vibrant spiritual life of the nation in a way that I experienced otherwise only in potentially divisive (though actually peaceful) political rallies on Battenberg Square promoted by the rival Blues and Reds: the Democrats and the Socialists. Of course it is true that dyed-in-the-wool former Communists never enter a church, but as the old prejudices fade and spitting matches fade in the memory, it is tempting for a West European to view the space below the dusky dome of Alexander Nevsky as a setting for the most important reconciliation that Bulgarians still have to achieve: among themselves.

Yet this memorial cathedral will always loom in central Sofia as a reminder of Big Brother to the East: five aisles remind you of all the great Russian cathedrals, their emphasis on vast spaces, divine power and majesty, the littleness of the human figure dwarfed by arches, vaults, and a complex of domes like aspects of the evening sky. The main dome soars to forty-six metres, mocking our insignificance and frailty.

If one feels uneasy about the anachronistic religious paintings in the Cathedral, icons within their true timespan can be seen in the cathedral's crypt, accessible from a door beside the main entrance. This is the Icon Gallery of the National

Art Gallery, with enough masterpieces to keep the iconnois-
seur dazzled for hours. Many icons were produced at Preslav
in ceramic form, but icon-painting on wood arose in Bulgaria
only during the Second Kingdom (1187-1396) when Veliko
Turnovo became a noted centre of religious art. A major work
of this period was the Christ Pantocrator with Apostles, a
double-sided icon from Nesebur officially 'under conservation'
but apparently, according to one official, not on show for
many years; another is an icon from Poganovo Monastery
dated about 1395 and showing the Virgin with St John the
Theologian on one side, and on the other the Vision of Ezekiel
and Habakkuk in Palaeologan style: dramatic, refined, atte-
nuated, with drapery as eloquent as a homily. This will shake
you out of your earthly preoccupations as shockingly as Ma-
saccio's Florentine Expulsion of Adam and Eve from Paradise. Magnificent icons, worthy to set beside those of Andrei
Rublyev or masterpieces in the Byzantine Museum in
Athens, include a 13th-century Virgin Hodigitria, a Virgin
Phaneromeni of 1541 from Sozopol, a Christ Pantocrator of
1607 from Nesebur, and 16th-17th altar doors from Veliko
Turnovo which mark the second phase of icon-painting, that
under Turkish dominion, such as a glowing, effeminate St
George (16th century) from Plovdiv, and a remarkable
Deiesis (1577) of unknown provenance. The decadence of
icon-painting dates from the 19th century, when whole
families, no matter how untalented, tried their hands at a
craft by now deemed patriotic, nationalistic, in aid of the political Revival. Since the Turks abhorred images of living
creatures, what could be greater in the sight of the Christian
God than the mass-production of icons? Of course, more
meant worse, and we understandably prefer SS. Theodore
Tiron and Theodore Stratilates (1614) from Dobursko village
to Zahari Zograf's tired-looking SS. Menas and Onufrius
(1845) from Dolnobeshovishki Monastery east of Vratsa.

The impressive Holy Synod (1910) near the Memorial Cathedral looks incongruous in the light of its period but not in
its architectural setting, nor in comparison with its contem-

*St Theodore Tiron and St Theodore Stratilates, an icon of 1614 in
the Icon Museum, St Alexander Nevski*

porary Theological Academy (1906), now Sofia University's Faculty of Theology with a rapid recent increase of students, across the pedestrian precinct from Sveta Nedelya. The reason you enter the academy is for its notable Ecclesiastical Historical-Archaeological Museum, a forbiddingly dry title concealing a brilliant abundance of art treasures, especially copies of murals outside Sofia which you might otherwise not have the chance to experience. Enchanting rocking-horse-like bas-reliefs portraying SS. George and Demetrius in painted wood from Sozopol make an intriguing icon dated back to the First Bulgarian Kingdom (10th-11th centuries). But of course this is unique, and the tradition will emerge in the Second Bulgarian Kingdom (13th-14th centuries), notably in Nesebur, Sozopol and Bulgarovo (Burgas district), areas subject to Greek influence in icon-painting and much else. From Bulgarovo we have hieratic images of Christ Pantocrator, who resembles God the Father in the Trinity more than God the Son, and a remarkable St Andrew. A beautifully-restored St Marina from Plovdiv is clothed in brilliant crimson against the ubiquitous golden background which simulates the wealth of Paradise. One astonishing double-sided Sozopol icon shows a writhing Christ Crucified on the reverse of a static Virgin with solemn Child. Papa Vitan of the Tryavna school was responsible for a scarcely more modern Virgin and Child (1837), without refined structure, perspective, or advances in colour; the same school produced a Last Supper brought here from Pirdop with barely-differentiated disciples and such an artificial composition that it enthrals by its primitivism. Miniature-painting was practised in monasteries, especially in Rila: here is a fine 15th-century St Luke from the Slepchenski Gospels. Woodcarving produced altar-doors from Arbanasi and Gumoshnik village. Goldsmiths such as Matei from Sofia made covers for Gospels from gilded silver.

119

25: CHURCHES

If Sveta Sofia boasts great antiquity, and Sveti Georgi complexity, Sveti Sedmochislenitsi the metamorphosis from a great mosque, and Sveta Petka Samarjiiska magnificent frescoes in a jewel-like setting, Alexander Nevski grandiose monumentality and the little Russian Church pirouetting fantasy, then Sveta Nedelya, the Church of the Holy Sabbath, represents the continuity of ecclesiastical tradition in Central Sofia from late Roman times, when the site formed the exact crossroads of classical Serdica. Shady trees give shelter to street vendors, nowadays bringing wares from Greece and Turkey as well as flowers and vegetables from market gardens in villages surrounding the capital. Trams flow and ebb around the church in a graceful curve: the traffic linking Bulevard Dimitrov with Vitosha and Stamboliiski buzzes all day long and into much of the night. A great Roman praetorium underlay this great church, which was dedicated in Ottoman times to Sveti Kral (Holy King), that is the Blessed King Stephen Urosh II Milutin of Serbia (1272-1321), whose remains were reputedly conserved within.

The old wooden and stone church was destroyed in 1856 but restored seven years later. After Liberation, the Russian architect A.N. Pomerantsev was commissioned to reconstruct it and it is his church that we see today, just as it is his Alexander Nevski and his Russian Church. After a Communist assassination attempt on King Boris III and his courtiers failed here in 1925, when a huge bomb detonated in the roof just before a state funeral service and a hundred and twenty innocent victims died, the building was restored by the group of D. Tsolov and I. Vasilyov. Luckily the terrorists did not destroy the miraculous carved iconostasis by Professor Travintski or the icons by Stanislav Dospevski of Samokov, which

Sveti Kral (now called Sveta Nedelya) before its damage by a Communist bomb in 1925

are overshadowed in quality by the immigrant Czech painter Jan Mrkvička's 'Last Supper'.

I sat on one of the few chairs, my gaze avoiding the unhappy modern murals by Nikolai Rostovtsev (1971-3), and watched two old ladies (Michelangelo's Cumaean and Persian Sibyls) deposit candles on the sputtering candelabra, mirroring the brevity of our life on earth. The brave new candles tossed their prodigal flames conceitedly above the veterans nearby, unconscious that all too soon their time would come.

One of my favourite churches in Sofia is dedicated to Sofia's own saint, Nikola, and was raised in 1911 to designs by Anton Tornyov, who also worked for a time on Sveti Georgi. This is eclecticism of a high order, selecting a frieze from Austro-Hungarian Sezession exuberance, classical elements, and what Pietro Scarpellini memorably called *bizantineggiante* style, that is to say not Byzantine, but of Byzantine

Sveti Nikola of Sofia. Rotating carved walnut columns (1911-22)

inspiration. A fine 'miracle-working' icon of the saint stands over the spot where he was reputedly martyred. Another pious account has the goldsmith Nikola stoned to death in 1511 for refusing to abjure his Christian faith on the steps of Sveti Kral (on the site of the present Sveta Nedelya).

Only the three chandeliers look out of place like a wineglass in a mosque. They are completely secular in intent, having been bought by King Ferdinand for his palace, then given to the church by King Boris III. Professor Margarita Koeva showed me over the church lovingly, for it possesses masterpieces of carving in walnut, highly polished and intricately worked over twelve years from 1911 to 1922 by the brothers Nestor and Lazar Alexiev from Debur. Interlaced vines entwine the polished columns, one of which rotates as the sacristan demonstrated. Professor Koeva escorted me behind the iconostasis, but a quacking priest flapped his black arms at us in excommunicative horror 'Ne mozhno!' (It's not allowed) – no women are permitted beyond the screen. I felt the same feminist fury that assails me on hearing of women imprisoned in Islamic fundamentalist societies for driving a car, or of women excluded from ordination to the priesthood by the Catholic Church. But against bigotry I act the coward, letting the sweep of misogynist history silence me too.

26: THE SYNAGOGUE AND JEWISH MUSEUM

Sofia's synagogue, the largest Sephardic synagogue in Europe, was designed by the Viennese architect Grunänger in the splendid Byzantine-Moorish style familiar from the great Viennese Sephardic synagogue destroyed during World War II. Sofia welcomed Jews in Roman times, but it only flourished as a Jewish centre after the expulsions from Spain and Sicily in 1492 and from Portugal five years later. In the 16th century the diaspora included Pleven and other communities expanded in Plovdiv, Burgas, Ruse, Varna, Shumen, Yambol, Kazanluk, Stara Zagora, Stanke Dimitrov and Lom.

Year after year, the yawning interior gathers dust as the promised reconstruction fails to materialise. Scaffolding hasn't been moved for months, buckets lie battered and empty, and your slightest whisper echoes as in a burial chamber. During the Ottoman period, Ashkenazi Jews came from Eastern Europe and the U.S.S.R. and it was a group of those who arranged for the building of the synagogue, commissioned from the same architect who created the Royal Palace on the site of the former Konak, or Ottoman administrative headquarters. The synagogue spreads under a massive dome, just behind the Hali or covered market, very near Banya Bashi Mosque.

Disappointingly, services for the small surviving Jewish community are held not beneath the impressive dome, but in a small side room with a grey wall-hanging from the defunct synagogue in the Danube city of Vidin, and another hanging presented by Dr S.D. Lessner of Nagasaki. Twenty-five to thirty Jews come here on Friday evenings and Saturday mornings, and up to a hundred on Jewish holidays and feast

Synagogue, from a postcard dated 1935

days but of the 50,000 Jews in Bulgaria before World War II, over 36,000 emigrated to Israel in 1948-9, and a trickle ever since has left a rump of scarcely 5,000 Jews in Bulgaria now.

Bulgaria had an excellent humanitarian record even when the Nazis tried to extradite Jews to concentration camps in their immediate sphere of influence, and despite the passing of the infamous anti-Semitic Protection of the Nation Act (1940), and a relatively low-key but vicious Kristallnacht. The Orthodox Church came out strongly against the Act, as did a number of distinguished writers, including Elizaveta Bagryana, Stilyan Chilingirov and Elin Pelin. Dedicated left-wing Jews had supported the Communists with their lives and dedicated work over many years, and they were to be supported in turn by many Communists, such as the distinguished academician Petko Stainov, and broadcasters of the underground radio station Hristo Botev, named for the revolutionary poet.

Documentation on the fate of Bulgarian Jews is displayed

in the permanent exhibition 'The Saving of the Bulgarian Jews' at 50 Bulevard Stamboliiski on Ploshtad Vuzrazhdane (closed on Saturdays). Beginning with the 2nd-century synagogue at Trajan's town of Oescus (near modern Gigen), the story of Bulgarian Jewry is illuminated by texts and pictures typified by Vasil Levski's stirring 'Rules for the Fighters for Bulgarian Liberation':

'The rule of Turkish masters shall be replaced by concord, fraternity and complete equality of all nationalities. Bulgarians, Turks, Jews and others shall be equal in faith, nationality, civil status and every other respect, all being ruled by the same law to be approved by the majority vote of all nationalities.'

Hitler's man in Sofia, Adolf Beckerle, in a letter to his bosses in Berlin dated 7 June 1943, attributed his lack of success in 'solving the Jewish problem' to 'the mentality of the Bulgarian people, who lack the ideological enlightenment that we have... A Bulgarian, having grown up together with Armenians, Greeks, Gypsies, does not find any faults with a Jew which could justify any special measures against him.'

Jews, settled mainly in the Yuchbunar (now Dimitrov) quarter of Sofia, left the city for the countryside; most were rescued by the arrival of Bulgarian partisans and the Soviet Army at the end of the War, on 9 September 1944, a date which gave its name to the square now renamed Alexander Battenberg which faces the Royal Palace.

The exhibition is captioned only in Bulgarian, but an excellent English-language illustrated book is available: *Saving the Jews in Bulgaria* (1941-1944).

The lady who showed me around was not herself Jewish; she looked tense and undernourished, perhaps anticipating the day when the museum would be closed and her livelihood sacrificed. Nobody had signed the visitors' book during the previous week.

27: DINNER WITH LIDIA

'Many men from the Western countries come to Bulgaria and like to marry Bulgarian women because we are very unusual for them: open heart, very moral and sparkling in the eyes, something which they can't find in their own country where all the women look the same. They may dress differently but if you look in their eyes they are all flat and lifeless: just the same as each other.' Lidia was speaking over dinner in the Restaurant Budapest at 145 Ulitsa Rakovski.

'On my mother's side, my great-grandfather was called An-eshti, 'Resurrected'. I find him interesting because he fought against the Turks, and was hacked into pieces when they killed him. My great-grandmother, a self-taught midwife, went to collect the small pieces to put them in the grave, that was in Kavalla now in Greece but at that time in Bulgaria. She speaks Greek, Bulgarian.'

'Give these violinists some money, otherwise they will never go away, and we can't hear ourselves think. That's better. The tune they play is "I don't want the daughter of a Sultan, just a little kiss from Anna."'

'My mother remembers life in Kavalla, but not very clearly. The family came back into the town of Gotse Delchev, in the far south of Bulgaria, named for the Macedonian freedom-fighter. My maternal grandfather was a men's tailor. My mother had four brothers, but one died when he was very little. He had a very appropriate name that boy: Angel. My grandmother died when I was two years old, in 1954. She was very saintly and beautiful, but my grandfather had four children to bring up, so he married again, a girl called Petra, who became a wonderful second mother to the children. She is still alive at the age of 81, but my grandfather died in 1986 at the age of 76.'

127

'Petra – daughter of a priest – worked in the tobacco fields, and I also remember going out into the fields to pick tobacco when I was young, from 4 to 8 a.m. to avoid the dew. When we got home again, all the family would sit down together in a circle, even my cousins, sorting tobacco. Then the leaves had to be dried outside the home; if it rained of course we had to bring the leaves inside again. Then the dried leaves were wrapped and sold at fixed prices to the government factory.'

'Our house in Gotse Delchev was big, with two storeys: two rooms downstairs and three upstairs. All the extended family lived there. Now they all have homes and families of their own, and only my grandmother and oldest uncle live there.'

'My father Delcho came from a poorer village, Ihtiman, east of Sofia, without any schools at that time. My paternal grandfather was called Tsvetan, or 'flower' and my grandmother Velika, meaning 'great'. They grazed sheep on the land round Ihtiman.'

'My father met my mother, Violetka, when he was an army captain quartered in Gotse Delchev in 1951, and they married there. I was born a year later, and lived in Sofia until 1961, when the army transferred my father to Plovdiv, where he stayed till 1965, then to the Army Academy in Moscow until 1967. I was studying Russian in a Russian school with other foreign children from Hungary and other socialist countries. Then when I came back to Sofia I attended the Russian Language School because I had the advantage of those two years, and finished it in 1970.'

'The first problem I had in my life was to live alone, in Sofia, when I became a student. My parents were still living in Plovdiv. It was difficult at that time living on my own because my male friends suddenly started to treat me as a woman not as a friend, but I thought of them still as friends, not just as men. So when I tried to take a moral stand, I lost all my men friends. Also, my girl friends I had left there in 1961 when I went to Plovdiv, just shortly after I had left the comfort of my family home. Also I started to speak against the Communists. I had problems with my father then, but now I agree with him. Then I felt frustrated because I couldn't go abroad – except to socialist countries. When I tried very hard to go, the Defence Ministry gave me permission to go to France, but my father stopped me.'

'Then I began higher education at the Mechanical Engineering Institute. It was a dilemma because I liked gymnastics, art, literature and chemistry too, but most of all I loved mathematics so engineering was a natural choice. I read a great deal of science fiction at that time (also nowadays) and I assumed that the syllabus would include space, and robots and all the fantasy that I had been reading about. I didn't really know what to expect, and after two years I wanted to give up but I had already passed the exams so it didn't make a lot of sense to change direction at that late stage. After I completed the course in 1976, I worked as a guide with Russian-speaking groups, because it was an agreeable alternative to working two months in agriculture, as we had to then. After my course I was assigned for three years to a Bulgarian-Hungarian company making lifts and cables, and suchlike. I was full of dreams, but it turned out to be heavy drudgery. Every day I had to wake at 5.30, begin work at 7.20 and finish at 4.10 and there was no time to change clothes, to go out, and besides I was very tired.'

'The work was very tiring. My boss used to come to me with a Japanese machine and say, 'Lidia, look this is very good, try to make one like this.' So I did it as a project and fulfilled his wishes for shall we say designing a special conveyor belt, which of course had to be efficient and very cheap. Then when I finished it and made it work efficiently, from cheap materials, he turned round to me and said, 'Oh, you are so young, did you think that nobody had discovered such a method before. We knew how to do such things twenty years before...' So I realised suddenly that the old man was frightened of me, because I was young, efficient, a woman, the new generation. I don't know what he thought, but he showed contempt for what I had done and I knew that in engineering I had no future, with bosses like that. It was easier to copy existing technology than to make our own new designs; I felt like a bird whose wings had been clipped. I couldn't try again. Then I lost my sleep, and I left my job.'

'I had a very airy, unrealistic view of engineering. In theory, there is no reason why a woman should not be able to do everything with machines. But when you come to do it, you realise that only men have the strength, and the understanding of machines, almost as if they are born with such a sense. A woman is never born with it, so if she learns this job very well, it will still be something foreign to her nature and her spirit. If you ask me, I should never allow women to do engineering. If you want to be a good mother and a good engineer, I should say this is too heavy for a woman, and you should not put yourself through all these troubles. Men always think of you first as a woman, then as an engineer: it is so much stress. My brother didn't finish technical education but he can repair everything, and I can repair nothing. I am not the only woman like this, I think.'

'I began to work as a guide again. In 1984 I met my future husband during fourteen days at Primorsko on the Black Sea coast, at the International Centre for Young People. He was a German-language guide there and I was a Russian-language guide with all girls from Russia. One of the Russian girls said to me, 'I like that Bulgarian man very much and I want you to talk to him and introduce me to him.' Well, I tried, but my husband only wanted to talk to me, and after this we got married, just one year later. My boy Viktor was born in 1986, and I stayed at home for three years to look after him.'

'My husband used to spend all our money on body-building and all his spare time too, so I never saw him. It was every weekend and every evening, straight from work. So in the end I said to him, "You must choose between me and your passion for body-building", even though I knew what his answer would be. Some time later he left, and he is still body-building furiously, like a man drugged, without a sensible mind of his own. He has left me with a son to bring up on my own, and he isn't paying me for the boy's expenses or the

Lidia Ivanova in the South Park

home. I don't know what he is doing now, but they say, the people who know him, that he is just spending more and more time improving his pectorals and so on.'

'I thought my future was in computers, but I was made redundant in October 1990, with two months on full pay at 250 leva, 90% the third month and 80% the fourth month, but never less than 165 leva (that was in the early months of 1991) plus government compensation changing all the time, plus 100 leva monthly for every child. Now the minimum is 37% of 620 leva plus 140 leva for each child, and of course the government adjusts these figures constantly.'

'If you ask me, I should think that 90% of Bulgarian girls would go abroad if they had the chance. I personally have the chance to go to France, but I still don't want to go. I am thinking not so much for myself but for Viktor, who should have a proper Bulgarian education. When he is old enough, he can make up his own mind whether he wants to emigrate, and when he can stand on his own two feet, I shall be free to make that decision too.'

28: SOFIA CONGRESS CENTRE

Formerly known as the National Palace of Culture, and abbreviated as such in Bulgarian to N.D.K. ('En-de-ka'), the newly-named Sofia Congress Centre is changing emphasis from mass culture to business and enterprise in the heady new world promised by a free market economy.

Far removed from Sofia's spartan apartment blocks of the 1960s in style and atmosphere, the Centre was created in 1981 to an octagonal plan on the ample Ploshtad Baba Nedelya which spreads out into welcoming gardens at the southern end of Bulevard Vitosha. The landscaped and pedestrianised precinct, where vendors supply candy floss, ice-cream, and pirated tapes of the Rolling Stones and Pink Floyd, possesses a metro station, booking centre, tourist office, restaurant and cafeteria perennially packed, a first-rate shopping arcade, bowling alley and discothèque. A bookshop offers Bulgarian classics, sometimes if you are lucky in translation, foreign authors in Bulgarian, and a request book where you can list books you want or have for sale, with your address or telephone number. How many blind dates have prospered on such flimsy pretexts?

Prior booking will assure you of a timed guided tour through this exciting building, beautiful, functional, and comfortable. I compared it with the roughly contemporary Barbican Centre in London, combining an exhibition centre with concert halls and a marvellous theatre with apron stage and perfect sightlines, where companies from La Scala, the Bolshoi have appeared, as have the Vienna Philharmonic and the London Symphony Orchestra.

The main building has eight floors above ground and three below, with a capacity in its twelve congress and conference halls ranging from 100 up to 3880, and all facilities for simultaneous translation and refreshments. Credit for the Naroden Dvorets na Kulturata goes to the architect Alexander Barov, responsible also for the curving Grand Hotel Sofia and Varna's festival complex.

The works of art selected for the N.D.K. fall into the nationalist-rhetorical style, out of synchrony with the progressive architecture surrounding them. The foyer's bronze figure of a young woman with flowing golden hair, her arms outstretched in a stiff gesture of welcome, is a symbolic representation of Sofia ('she grows, but doesn't grow old' is the city motto) by Dimitur Boikov. A tapestry by Marin Varbanov provocatively jumbles various Bulgarian works of art in sharp and clashing juxtaposition that seems to reduce the impact of each one, by snatching it out of context.

Time and again one notices the technical brilliance of acoustics, lighting, and equipment while regretting the artistic levels of ceramic tiles by Vanko Urumov, a sub-Blakean mural of 'The Ascent of Bulgarian Culture' by the academic Dechko Uzunov, and a sub-Rivera view of 'Man and Peace', discordant in colour and composition, by Yoan Leviev. Another flawed work is Hristo Stefanov's mural 'Fire', which desperately crams 43 historical figures and six symbols into one space without tact, proportion or sensitivity.

As a space the centre scores significantly, with comfortable seats for major screenings of new overseas films such as Bertolucci's *The Last Emperor*, memorable orchestral occasions, and epochmaking events such as the 23rd General Congress of Unesco in 1985.

More depressing is the recent tendency to fill the corridors and foyers with pinball games, space invaders, and other electronic *kitsch* which admittedly appeal to the younger generation here, just as one regrets the ubiquitous pachinko parlour or karaoke saloon in contemporary Japan. The 'Palace of Culture', once a temple to Bach and Beethoven, is now filled with stalls offering clothes and radios, toys and videocassettes, pornography and shoes. Then I remember: newfound freedoms must include the freedom to disnefy oneself, to break free of all constraints of official taste and morality. State-subsidised high culture must either be rethought or abolished altogether, leaving the cultural desert that induced Arthur Miller to abandon Broadway for London when offering the première of his latest play. Free enterprise includes the freedom to ditch one's high culture and assume the mantle of other people's vulgarity. I picked up the once-reputable *Edna Sedmitsa v Sofia* ('One Week in Sofia') and found three bare-breasted young ladies on the front page.

Old women in black sitting outside the modern palace will cast their minds back to their youth, when this open space accommodated a flea market and fruit and veg stalls as well as a barracks.

Black leather jackets are the uniform of the young and the middle-aged: they say 'I'm ready to do a deal, buying, selling, exchanging currency, whatever you want'. Some girls flounce in black leather skirts or shorts of truly awful vulgarity. The pity of it is that the girls themselves would be ravishingly beautiful with slinkily cut silk-black hair, without cheap make-up clumsily over-applied to mask their natural beauty. A girl told me that when her mother wore a mini-skirt to school during the Communist period she had had her knees rubberstamped by a zealous headmistress.

As I sat on a bench a Bulgarian covertly reading a book straightened up when he noticed me. 'You are a foreigner', he said, 'can you read this?' I took the volume, bound without a title on spine or cover and translated aloud *The Beginning of the Third Kingdom,* by Stefan Nikolov Stambolov, with a foreword by Dimitur Markov, published in 1898 by Marinov.

'That's right. Every copy of this book but the one I possess was destroyed by the Communists.'

'But Stambolov was the kingmaker, appointed with his brother-in-law Mutkurov and Karavelov by Alexander Battenberg when he left Bulgaria in 1886.'

'That's right. It was Stambolov who appointed Vasil Radoslavov as caretaker prime minister before the holding of a new grand national assembly. That assembly would have re-elected Battenberg if they could, but it didn't vote for any alternative, and it was Stambolov who persuaded Ferdinand of Saxe-Coburg-Gotha to accept an election by the assembly of July 1887, and arrive in Bulgaria in August. It was Stambolov who won over the Orthodox Church to Ferdinand, despite his Catholicism. It was Stambolov who pushed through a constitutional change enabling the devoutly Catholic wife of Ferdinand, Marie-Louise, to bring up her children as Roman Catholics.'

Stambolov is a non-person in Bulgaria even today, having been assassinated in 1895, a year after being dropped by King Ferdinand, at the hands of a vengeful Macedonian. His book on the early days of the reign of Ferdinand would be very welcome in translation, as would a reprint in Bulgarian.

29: THE EMBARRASSING GIFT

As Eastern European countries bounce painfully downhill from an economy of low salaries and low costs to lower salaries and higher costs, followed by unemployment and even higher costs, travelling westerners feel obliged to bring gifts.

The embarrassment in Sofia – as in Petersburg or Warsaw – comes from the fact that your host will feel awkward about receiving gifts at all, and silently offended if the gifts are inappropriate or unwanted. Take the case of toiletries: shampoos, conditioners and scents often in short supply, but periodically coming on to the market in bewildering abundance like desert plants after rain. 'Do you think we can't keep ourselves clean?' is the unspoken rebuff as the lady unwraps expensive toilet soap.

I like to pack scarves and gloves, tights and panties, for a hostess who has produced an unexpected meal, only for a host to wonder 'Why is he thinking about my wife's underclothes?'

Food of one's own country, such as fine chocolate or whisky, is quickly consumed and forgotten, and Sofia still produces a great variety of wines and spirits; further, you don't want to imply that your hosts cannot eat properly at home when they have just proved the opposite.

Cigarettes are a national addiction, but why should one deliberately set out to shorten the lives of those who have offered you friendship and hospitality, even if they so wish?

Books and records, cassettes and pictures all make acceptable presents, but contriving to fit the present to the recipient as you would at home can be tricky, if many of the recipients will be almost unknown to you.

Trickiest of all is the gift of money, whether leva or hard currency. For a stranger, little pride will be at stake when services have been rendered; but the closer the friend, the more embarrassing it will become, and the amount a matter for agonising calculation. I always wrap up the notes in a letter of thanks and seal it in an envelope, so take plenty of paper and envelopes with you because both are in short supply, to the point where schoolchildren must now provide their own notebooks because schools have run out and cannot buy any more. That is the reason for the little piles of exercise-books on sidewalk-stalls and street corners, where those who have cornered the market sell one notebook at a time to students who would otherwise go without.

So why not take a supply of notebooks? I suppose because if I were a parent presented with three notebooks to divide between four children, I should feel humiliated that through no fault of my own, or theirs, or my country's, I could not afford to give them the necessary supplies in a culture which has always justifiably prided itself on free education.

Women sometimes go through several abortions, so the provision of good-quality condoms or other contraceptive devices in sufficient quantities should be acceptable, but I personally baulk at pulling out a supply confronted with the gaze of three or four close friends, not to mention what my wife would think if I casually explained that 'they are not intended for my own use'. I suppose I lack the brashness necessary for explaining to customs officers my need for sixty condoms during a fortnight's stay in Sofia. I have never been asked to open my baggage by Bulgarian customs officials as a matter of fact, but the dread remains uppermost in my mind.

And when I approached the whole matter logically, writing for advice about what my hosts lack, most embarrassingly of all there was utter silence from their side. *Asking* is what I meant; *begging* is what they felt.

I took packets of teabags, though few Bulgarians drink tea, and jars of instant coffee, in spite of the fact that most Bulgarians prefer to grind their own beans or drink stronger brews. I felt again that anguish that comes upon foreigners in Sofia who try to reciprocate the kindness that they always meet: Bulgarians are naturally inclined not to receive, but to give. This generosity of theirs is the most embarrassing gift of all.

30: SOFIA HUNTING MUSEUM

As in most countries of Eastern Europe, hunting and angling in Bulgaria have for millennia provided vital meat and fish protein for the local population. The first formal hunters' congress took place in 1898, when sixty-six informal hunting societies decided to form a union called 'Sokol', after the union's emblem: a falcon. Anglers held their first congress in 1929, and the two unions merged in 1947.

The Union of Hunters and Anglers has grandiose headquarters at Bulevard Vitosha 31-33, with fine tapestries befitting its status as the only representative body for 60,000 hunters and 120,000 anglers, whose subscription to the union entitles them to practise these sports.

Visitors are welcome at the museum, founded here in 1982 to show the main species and the most valuable trophies, including the world record *cervus elaphus,* and the second *dama dama,* after the Hungarian champion. The last four records for wild cat are Bulgarian, as is the current record for wild boar, until recently held by Poland. Jackals, foxes, brown bear, moufflon: here are spectacular stuffed animals and dioramas of a deer family in winter and small game, including pheasant and partridge. Only a tenth of the exhibits can be displayed at any one time.

I met Mrs Rossitsa Zlatanova, Deputy Chairwoman of the Hunters' and Anglers' Union, and absolute world champion at casting in 1976, 1978 and 1980. To join, one must take practical and theoretical examinations, including gun-handling and safety measures, at any one of the hundred or so regional branches. Possession of guns is controlled by the Union, and you can only hunt free of charge in your own home district. An annual combined licence is 55 leva, with a fee of 45 leva for hunting only, and 25 leva for only angling.

Rossitsa Zlatanova

The union is rich because it demands service from members in the form of work, such as the care of game, breeding fish, and selling game and fish on the open market, buying and exporting furs, and supplying guns and rods and all other fishing tackle. Local hunters prefer migrating birds, wild boar, pheasants and deer; foreign hunters come mainly from Germany, Greece, Italy, France and Spain, and book their trips either through their own local firms or direct with Balkantourist, 1 Bulevard Vitosha. The season for aquatic game, fallow deer and stags runs for 5 months from 1 September; for wild goat and moufflon for 4 months from 1 September; for bears for 3 months from 1 October. Trout may be fished from 1 February for 8 months, and all other fish from 1 June to 15 April.

I asked Rossitsa about the effects of the changes after the events leading to the downfall of Todor Zhivkov.

'The State Hunting Grounds kept for the private use of former leading comrades were liquidated, but the Union possessed no such private grounds, so we were not affected. By an Extraordinary Congress, executive members were elected in a different way. That is, candidates were suggested by the members. But of course, the economic crisis has its own consequences. Members tend to hunt during the season for food, not just for sport or trophies. Unlike in the west, hunters had no august social standing: they were just ordinary people like you and me. We have many more animal species than highly urbanised societies like Germany or Belgium, and the quantities of those species tend to be much higher. We have between 800 and 900 brown bears. Wolves come during the viciously cold periods from Romania and Turkey.'

'Does poaching exist?'

'The State Committee on Forests check that no hunting occurs in the close season. Our members exercise a great deal of self-control. Poaching exists, of course, but one can say it's on a small scale, and anyone caught is expelled from the Union.'

'What is your background?'

142

'I was born in 1945 in Sofia, graduated from Sofia University as an economist and worked in foreign trade. My husband has a private company now. We have two children: my son is 24 and has emigrated to Germany; my daughter is 13. I should say that hunting and angling are passions in Bulgaria, and I believe they will become even more popular when ordinary people can enjoy more leisure for such pursuits.'

31: THE OPERATIC MADMAN

We are all crazy in our egotism, our prejudices, our barely uncontrollable assertions at every point: 'I am right', 'You are wrong' blazed across every political debate, every act of terrorism, every correspondence page of every newspaper. In a hundred years, our pet passions will be forgotten; a hundred miles away they are ignored even as we speak.

So perhaps the best crazes are just the least offensive, the least intolerant. Like train-spotting, fossil-hunting, stamp-collecting. And opera.

I have been crazed about opera since I first heard John Hargreaves as Don Giovanni at Sadler's Wells in 1955, Jon Vickers in *The Trojans* at Covent Garden, Hans Hotter as Wotan in the *Ring,* and the great Bulgarian bass Boris Christoff as Boris Godunov on 1 June 1961. Afterwards we stood together inside the stage door, both still overcome by the final scene, where the Russian Tsar sinks dying with the words 'Bozhe! Smyert! Prosti menya!' (God! Death! Forgive me!) and points out his son to the assembled boyars: 'Vot! Vot vash Tsar! Prostitye... prostitye' (There! There is your Tsar! Have mercy... have mercy...). Since then I have haunted stage doors for autographs of the great singers after the last of the fashionably-attired audience have dispersed.

The National Opera of Bulgaria has given the world dozens of its greatest voices, mainly in the Russian and Italian repertory. Who will ever forget the Salomé of Borisovo-born Lyuba Welitsch (the German form of Velich), Mariana Radeva at Zagreb Opera, Elena Nikolai at Rome Opera, Ghiaurov and Ghiuselev, Kabaivanska and Tomova-Sintov, Savova and Dimitrova, Evstatieva and Mineva, Uzunov and Venkov? Every generation seems to produce a Bulgarian genius and many singers of international calibre: Veneta

Yaneva, Dimitur Stanchev, Kaludi Kaludov, Alexandrina Milcheva, Hristina Angelakova, Valerie Popova and now her daughter-pupil Alexandrina Pendachanska.

Communist countries always treated opera as high culture to be subsidised for the masses, like theatre and ballet or great literature of the correct political tint, so tickets to the public cost less than a dollar, and frequent allocations were made so that schoolchildren, the military, students, leading politicians and members of trade unions could get in free. Singers received small salaries in return for massive fringe benefits and security of employment.

The same subsidy system has also applied to operetta. Operettas by such as Lehar and Lortzing and musicals such as *My Fair Lady* are performed except during the summer holiday season at the Stefan Makedonski State Musical Theatre at 4 Bulevard Volgograd, near the Levski Monument. The German-style repertory system means that you could see five different operettas on five successive evenings, invariably to a very high professional standard.

With the freeing of the market, all these conditions favourable to cheaply accessible opera and operetta have disappeared overnight, and Bulgarian opera singers have found themselves thrown upon an overcrowded world stage. Well-known stars earn fabulous fees as guests in Los Angeles or La Scala; singers with excellent voices but little recognition overseas have a glum future.

So every night at Sofia Opera is an adventure. The programme is printed in two parts: one is the permanent cover, with a brief outline of the plot and description of the composer's life and works; the other is a hastily-compiled sheet with that evening's cast, often altered in pen just before the curtain goes up. As in operetta, the German repertory-system has always been adopted in Bulgaria opera houses so that several singers study each rôle, and the cast can be shuffled according to availability. Each conductor generally conducts every work. Productions tour the country, and may linger in the repertory for many years without substantial change.

The risk factor is low, and avant-garde productions currently so outraging audiences in Germany, the U.K. and the Netherlands are virtually unknown. This means that audiences quickly become deeply familiar with favourites such as *Aïda, Il Trovatore* or *La Bohème,* but are completely ignorant of 90% of the repertory familiar in the West, since few shops even stock the records, cassettes and compact discs taken for granted elsewhere, for lack of hard currency.

At *Madama Butterfly,* Valerie Popova had been replaced at the last minute by Daniela Nedyalkova. The stalls were buzzing with old friends greeting each other. 'Shalom', waved an old Jewish gentleman, nattily attired in a gray suit with waistcoat, to a Jewish couple sitting straight-backed and solemn in the seats next to mine. Embarrassed Japanese men who had not understood the seat-numbering eventually found their seats in the centre of the front row, where their view would be obscured by the gesticulations of the conductor, Boris Hinchev.

At the farthest right-hand seat in the front row a bright, twittering little woman in her late fifties sat chirping out of her senses, nodding in time to music in her head. Clearly well-known to the timpanist, just below her in the pit, she made stage-whispered, emergency appeals for him to take a note she had hurriedly scribbled. 'Take it', she muttered, 'it's for Mitko'. Dimitur is one of the commonest of all Bulgarian names, and she might have referred to any male musician past or present, or chorus-member, or stage-hand.

Rows of private-faced Bulgarians gazed with polite interest at the nervous Japanese in front of them. The audience gossiped and flicked through the inexpensive programme quickly. We felt conscious of the eyes of the circle and gallery upon us. Professor Yosifov of the Opera administration entered his box stage left. Puccini's overture began.

At the interval, no drinks or coffee could be found. A few men ambled along to the toilet, but most bolted outside as quickly as possible: smoking is allowed outside.

When the performance was over, and bouquets presented

Daniela Nedyalkova, backstage at Sofia Opera

147

to Nedyalkova as a dazzling Cio-Cio-San and Ivanka Ninova as an affecting Suzuki, I waited in the little hall opening on to Bulevard Dondukov, beside the porter's glassed-in enclosure. The bird-woman sat bolt upright, smiling in recollected delight at that beloved *Un bel dì*. Friends had come with bunches of wild flowers to greet the stars. I took up an unobtrusive position on a chair in the corner. As master of ceremonies, taking up most of one bench, a quavering baritone in his late seventies was singing old Bulgarian folk songs off key, while absently pulling off the heads of assorted flowers in his spray of chrysanthemums. 'Those were the days', he said, 'when they did Weber's *Der Freischuetz*. I sang in the chorus so you could hear me on the other side of Vitosha. The stage-doorhand pointedly turned over the pages of *Duma* and held them up in front of his face, to ward off conversation.

'Lalala, lalala, LALALA LA LAAAAA' enthused the staring madman, whose only audience now could be found far from any stage. Chrysanthemum petals dropped as from the wild fingers of Ophelia. We waited, embroiled in our uncommunicative silence, hoping for a respite.

'Songs from Pirin', he announced, with a portentous wave undermined by giggles, 'ma in *Ispagna* son già mille e tre, that's a lot of women, Leporello.' I shrank visibly, and by now the desultory conversations had fallen silent, as all eyes turned towards the running commentary on operas past. I don't know whether I expected him to invite Donna Elvira to come to the window, or to slay the Commendatore. Then a flutter and a bustle, and the night's stars emerged together to be greeted by their friends. But Popeye, not to be outdone, seized Daniela Nedyalkova's wrist and bowed before offering her the chrysanthemums. 'What's your name, dearie?' he stage-whispered.

'Daniela', responded Cio-Cio-San with a charming smile, concealing her embarrassment.

He drew himself up to his full height, and with a playful twist of the wrist declared, 'I am Pinkerton – returned!'

32: CENTRAL RAILWAY STATION

One of the successful buildings of the 'Seventies in Sofia is Panchev's Kristal Restaurant (1975) at 119 Rakovski, between the Sofia and Bulgaria Hotels; another is Zhekov's irregular and idiosyncratic Sofia Drama Theatre (1977). But the most successful of all, airy, roomy, and super-efficient, is the Central Railway Station ('Tsentralna Gara' is the sign on buses, not to be confused with 'Stochna Gara', or Goods Station) of 1975.

Watching behaviour at railway stations is the simplest method of judging a nation's character: the messy cacophony and superb *cappuccino* at Bologna to the smooth efficiency

Central Railway Station

and *Wurst* at Wiesbaden. In Greek trains, bread and olives emerge as soon as the train chugs out of the station. At Bombay's Victoria Terminus several hundred bodies seem to converge on one seat as if by karmic predestination. At Sofia Central Station I sit and wait for passengers. One fat fellow in a raincoat bearing a transistor radio listens intently to Engelbert Humperdinck's 'Please release me, let me go' as he trudges slowly past. A woman of thirty quickly pats her hair charmingly, needlessly, to draw fatal attention to its raven-black beauty. A crowd gathers in a semi-circle around an American evangelist whose finely-tuned translator chants mystical words of salvation to wide-eyed but essentially cynical individuals not easily fooled. The underground concourse pulsates with private enterprise, with pirated tapes of Madonna or the Pet Shop Boys, popcorn-vendors, trinket-stalls, and a proliferation of newspapers in a society hungry for different aspects of truth. Soft drinks here; open sandwiches with cheese or salami there. Flowers already wrapped in little bunches. Umbrellas. Cheap watches. Vodka and whisky. American cigarettes. Ice-cream. A wave of half-exposed magazines, some titillatingly semi-erotic, amid the solid socialist *Trud* and *Duma*. A little farmer in an ill-fitting suit glances about him apprehensively: they don't have underground concourses in the Rhodope mountains. Two boys play tag around the columns. A dramatically sullen beauty in a maroon coat creates a Marlene Dietrich look with slighty-lifted eyebrows and shoulders oblique to the throng: yes, Svetla, we all covet you. Two old women, plainly sisters, bump into each other in another attempt to become the Siamese twins their mother always wanted. Would one be seeing the other off, both heartbroken at another parting, away from confidences, black coffee, and endless gossip, to a husband silent in his world of hunting, fishing and smoke?

Indicator boards laconically bear the numbers of romance: Moscow due 15.20, Svoge due 17.12, Pleven due 17.30, Varna due 17.40, Kyustendil due 17.42, Plovdiv due 18.03, Vidin/Lom due 20.05.

150

33: THE CITY OF TRUTH

I walked with Dr Krassen Stanchev of Ecoglasnost around the empty Battenberg Square, still silently echoing to 'Communism is Retreating, Sleep Peacefully Children', performed as a group ritual during that curious phenomenon, the City of Truth I asked Krassen how the City began.

'In December 1989, Petar Mladenov, who had ousted Zhivkov with the Kremlin's prior approval, was heard to say about a pro-Democracy demonstration, 'We had better use tanks', a sentence recorded on videocamera. The demonstration called for an immediate change to article 1 of the Constitution which legalised the supremacy of the Communist Party. Ex-President Mladenov accused the reporter of forgery, which so incensed the democrats that they demanded his resignation. This they achieved by the simple and rather ingenious method of establishing a new form of democracy: a city of tents in the centre of the totalitarian triangle of Sofia: the Party Headquarters on Lenin Square, the Dimitrov Mausoleum, and the Presidency just beyond the Bulgarian National Bank. The location of these hundreds of informal, democratic, even illegal tents seemed crucially symbolic to Sofia and the country as a whole. It was as if the life force was draining from the buildings which established Communist control, and was revitalising each night the motley collection of campers: artists, students, intellectuals, and ordinary people who had suffered under Communism. Our 'city' had its mayor and municipal government, its own recognised informal streets, church, library, and open central square. It became a recognised Communism-free zone for evening strolls, when money would be collected, and food brought by sympathisers. The City of Truth toppled Mladenov, the crypto-Communist, and survived even after the elec-

151

tion of a new President. It will be seen as a magical and incandescent moment in the history of Bulgarian democracy. It all ended with the ceremonial setting on fire of the Communist headquarters, when the people danced with joy, and the militia stood around powerless to intervene in the euphoria of the time. Of course, the burning was merely symbolic and no lives were lost. The building still stands, as you will see. But the moment is carved in our memories.'

Communist Party headquarters, after damage by democrats

Vaclav Havel, who would have camped in the city if born a Bulgarian, calls his own experiment in Czechoslovakia *Living with Truth,* but I take it that he means by this the attempt to remove our veils of ignorance, prejudice, unawareness, negligence, or stubbornness. He means that we should continually open ourselves and each other to new possibilities. For what is 'truth' if overthrow of one lie may itself become a lie to the next generation when defended too aggressively or subjectively, at that moment when we attempt to silence opponents who hold any different opinion.

Countless millions of leva disappeared during the period of Communist rule, and putting Zhivkov on trial was a device to avoid the issue by seizing and humiliating a scapegoat to prevent wider investigations. Such investigations may be held later, but they have a way of being dropped because so many rank and file, so many leaders and bosses were implicated: if more than half the country could be considered culpable by supporting the Communist regime, how could you set about indicting, sentencing and imprisoning more than half the population? Put in these terms, it is a miracle that the Democrats were ever elected to power in the first place. A fact to remember is that many of the wealthiest and most influential of the new administrators and industrialists, bankers and bureaucrats, teachers and judges have a past they would rather conceal, transform or forget. The next *History of Bulgaria* will probably not name many names.

34: SHOPPING

Paradoxically, Bulgaria is too full of cheap goods to be recommended as a shopper's paradise. The reason is that during the Communist yoke (and that applies equally to Russia, to Poland, to Romania, to Albania) centralized planning ignored the needs of the consumer, so that the wrong goods were produced, by workers so badly paid that they could take no pride in their work. Full employment guaranteed jobs for even the most appalling botchers, and the talented moved up into administrative positions, leaving manufacturing processes to those who could not do the job properly. Without adequate equipment, investment for modernisation, market research, motivation or comparison with comparable goods from other countries, the only advantage of Communist-made goods lay in their cheapness. But this too was illusory, because their prices, assigned by the State, bore no relation to the cost of manufacture. They could not be exported because their quality would be ridiculed by overseas buyers; the domestic market did not find the goods cheap because the average national wage stayed artificially low. Housewives in Communist states became adept at making and mending, preserving fruit and vegetables in seasonal supply, queueing, and above all simply doing without. How often have I heard Bulgarian women say, half-defensively, 'Of course I have to feed the children and my husband first', as though they were officially and unofficially recognised as Second-Class Citizens, brainwashed into street-cleaning and tram-driving, taking on extra jobs as if in duty bound.

Heartbreakingly, it is now the women who are again required to tighten their belts as goods fail to arrive in the shops, or stay in short supply, or rise astronomically in price beyond their budget. A market's freedom may merely prolong

Central Open-Air Market

the housewife's servitude. She survives by 'the network': that interlocking sequence of friendships and relationships, visits and gifts, bargains and barters, which alone makes life tolerable. After all, they are all in the same boat and if it were to sink we should all perish. So it must stay afloat. If invited out for a meal, you take a gift equivalent to the value of the meal or more. Not because it is expected, but because it forms a natural link in the chain of 'the network'. On one side there is the tiny minority of the nomenklatura, that corrupt network of high-ranking officials in the Government, Big Business, Commerce, Banking, the Foreign Service, and tourist agencies or companies with access to hard currency, and an influence far greater than their numbers would suggest. On the other side is the vast mass of people without hard currency, without connections inside the nomenklatura, who have to survive by the network and have an influence far smaller than their numbers would suggest. Luckily, in Sofia,

155

most families are connected with villages across the country where fruit and vegetables are grown, where meat is available, where game can be shot and fish caught. Vineyards will recover under private ownership, tobacco crops will bring in cash, and animals such as sheep, goats and pigs can be kept around the chickenrun.

Foreign travel restrictions were lifted in early 1989 and Bulgarians with an external passport were permitted to travel to the towns just over the border, and to change the equivalent of about £33 (US$60) into foreign currency. They could then of course 'shop' abroad, and bring in items much dearer in Bulgaria or unobtainable there. Smuggling was rife, and quite understandable, because £33 represented a year's salary at the time, and many ingenious entrepreneurs had managed to acquire even more than £33 to exchange against coveted purchases...

Since the coup against Todor Zhivkov later in 1989, private enterprise has flourished as never before, and the vitally important black economy is noticeably less officiously persecuted. Regular coaches shuttle between Sofia and capitalist centres such as Istanbul and Edirne (Odrin on the Bulgarian posters), Athens and Thessaloniki. For the cost of the fare and an overnight hotel, adventurous Bulgarians can bring back for resale a range of goods much wider than Bulgaria can herself yet produce, or the same goods of a much better quality. Vendors display their wares on the ground, on packing-cases, on carts or stalls, wherever passers-by can see them. In a sense, the most interesting shopping in Bulgaria is no longer to be found in the shops at all, but outside.

As the streets gradually filled up with vendors and their stalls, many of them ordinary people needing to sell some possessions to augment the weekly budget, the Mayor of Sofia banned street vendors by decree. So in the Kristal Park on Bulevard Ruski the open-air artists at their easels were removed, to be replaced by a forlorn stall with a petition which you could sign pleading with the Mayor to let the artists have their park back. I then found some of these same artists in the square around the Alexander Nevski Memorial Cathedral, pursuing free enterprise and art in the open air to typify the ingenuity of the Bulgarian spirit faced with adversity.

The mother of all department stores in Bulgaria is Sofia's Tsentralen Universalen Magazin, the Central Universal Department Store, open from 8 a.m. to 8 p.m. next to the Sheraton Sofia on Sveta Nedelya Square. Impressions are relative, and nobody would think of comparing TsUM to Bloomingdale's or Harrod's, but relative to Albania or Romania I found that Bulgarians had a good deal to spend and a wide choice of goods without the need for hard currency. Prices have risen dramatically, and government levels of compensation have failed to keep pace, but at least everyone in the 'Gastronom' could find enough to eat, and the clothes departments provided enough decent clothes for men, women and children, though fashions remain behind the times, colours drab, and

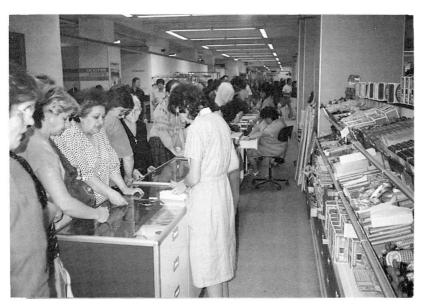

Inside TsUM (1991)

quality poor. Women were more numerous at counters offering fabrics to make up than at racks of ready-made garments. The sewing-machine is every Bulgarian woman's standby at times of wear and tear. The ground floor showed pottery and flowers, simple handicrafts like large wooden bowls and colourful folksy embroidered blouses, cardigans of mediocre quality, and fur jackets old-fashioned in style but very inexpensive.

Queues stayed good-natured, without shoving, shouting, or attempts to gain illicit precedence. Women buying cloth called for bolts from the shelf, and felt the stuff thoughtfully. Those who had made up their mind were given sales-slips, which they took to a cashier's queue, and paid over the money in exchange for a rubber-stamp on the sales-slip, which was then brought back to the sales assistant. A third girl had wrapped the purchase, which was handed over. TsUM still suffers to a large extent from seller's syndrome, that quirk of Communist life which decreed that customers should think themselves lucky to find anything in the shops at any price. Why make anything attractive, or package it beautifully, when there is no competition? If you judge a civilisation by the quality of its packing, Japan emerges as the clear victor, and Albania at the tail-end, with Bulgaria towards the relegation zone, with Romania and Poland.

Department stores similar to TsUM can be found between Vitosha, Positano and Alabin (Trade Centre), at 16 Bulevard Dimitrov (Sofia) and at 58-62 Bulevard Vitosha (Valentina). Children's department stores are at 4 Bulevard Stamboliiski (Detmag) and on Ulitsa 3 April (Yan Bibiyan, named for a children's fictional hero in a book by Elin Pelin).

The most wondrous of all shopping centres in Sofia is the National Revival-style Hali, borrowing its name from Les Halles, the covered market in Paris. It was created in 1909-11 to designs by Torbov and in its ornate splendour gloomy drab-scarfed grannies incongruously hauled shopping baskets laden with beer and mineral water, sugar, and non-alcoholic soft drinks of dubious ingredients, milk, biscuits, frozen meat joints and chicken, eggs, tinned fish and mayonnaise, queueing at twenty tills. Internally, it was reconstructed on the open-plan method to allow more light to irradiate Piranesi-like shadows. But the municipality rashly decided to close it for reconstruction a couple of years back, and the sudden recession dealt works a blow from which they have yet to recover. If and when it reopens, it may well still be the most atmospheric of Sofiote shopping centres, reminding one of those glorious Victorian markets in India, such as the Crawford Market in Bombay or the Ray Market in Pune.

Shops are opening and expanding all over Sofia as the old monopolies crumble and entrepreneurs make deals with local and international suppliers. Special souvenir shops can be found at the former National Palace of Culture, Sredets at 7 Ul. Lege, on Vitosha Bulevard, 42 Ul. Alabin, and at 6 Bul. Blagoev. Sports goods are at 13 Vitosha and carpets at 41 Vitosha. Leather goods, often excellent buys, can be found at Vihren, 5 Iskursko Chaussée, 32 Tolbuhin, 9 Slaveikov, and 4 Ruski, the last-named being the shop of the Arts and Crafts Guild, for applied arts. For knitwear I recommend Yanitsa at 61 Vitosha and Ruen at 50 Alabin. For cottons try 45 Tolbuhin and for linens Perun at 42 Dondukov. Semi-precious minerals are sold at Mineralsouvenir, 10 Ruski, and crystal and china at Quartz, 8 Vitosha. The Bulgarian Numismatic Association is at 1 Ul. Solunska and the Union of Bulgarian Philatelists at 15 Bul. Traikov, where there is one of several philatelic shops, others being at 7 Blagoev, the Central Rail Station, TsUM and the Sofia Department Store.

Among record shops, I can recommend one in the basement of the National Palace of Culture, and others on Ploshtad Slaveikov, 10 Ruski, 38 Stamboliiski, 29 Dimitrov and 2 Vazov. Czech records are to be found in the Czech Shop at 100 Rakovski near the Kristal Garden. For secondhand books try Letostrui near the British Embassy and the stalls and shops on Ploshtad Slaveikov, 6 Ruski, 10 Ruski, 9 Vitosha and 32 Dondukov. Vendors on many pavements and gardens offer excellent new and secondhand books, including the dictionaries that were once so scarce and are now sold at a premium to those who can afford them. Music scores are at 151 Rakovski, and specialised bookshops exist for architecture (5 Tolbuhin), literature (7 Kunchev) and medicine (32 Vitosha). My favourite haunt for books is the underpass facing Sofia University.

For paintings and graphics the Union of Bulgarian Artists' Art Gallery at 6 Shipka is the venue for changing exhibitions, and the administrative staff will gladly put you in touch with artists on show. Table-top sculpture and the decorative arts are among the strongest media for Bulgarian artists, who number among them great textile artists and printmakers, still underpublicised and undervalued by Western dealers and galleries. Commercial galleries, often with variable criteria of quality, are emerging ubiquitously, often with inflated prices that might well be subject to negotiation.

Here is my short-list of souvenirs from Bulgaria representing the best value, remembering that Bulgarian wine is freely available abroad: records, cassettes, music scores, illustrated books, leatherware, tablecloths and napkins, embroidery, ceramics, paintings and graphics, wooden bowls, dishes and spoons, and textile art. What a shame that yoghourt doesn't travel!

35: SIMEONOVO

Sofia has 12,000 hectares of parks and gardens, of which the Park na Svoboda (Freedom Park) laid out in 1882 accounts for 420 and the post-World War II South Park accounts for a further 560.

The tram-ride out to the Pioneers' Palace, where Communist youth went for leisure and indoctrination, passes through wooded parkland. At the Pioneers' Palace, you get off and change to a bus for Simeonovo, if you want to explore the new Zoopark, moved from a position closer to the city centre in recent years. The Zoopark (off Simeonska Chaussée) is open daily from 8.30 to 7 p.m. Captions on enclosures are in Bulgarian, with scientific names rendered in Latin. Some animals are shut up in confined spaces, but the grizzly bear and the Kodiak bear possess great open spaces, and thrive on food hurled in the air towards them by entranced visitors. Emus run around in their new landscape, but the Wild Cat House I found depressingly small for tiger, leopard, lynx and caracal. A pair of Indian elephants and a pair of African rhinoceroses divided the attentions of a party of Maltese tourists on their way from Luqa Airport to Poland. Due to a faulty connection, they have time to explore Vitosha and the National History Museum as well as this Zoopark before continuing to Warsaw, Cracow and Zakopane, and I found friends and neighbours of mine from Senglea, that stone village jutting into Grand Harbour on Malta. Families enjoyed ice-creams, cold drinks, and double-seated canopied bicycles, which they were joyfully racing along the wide, level streets of this modern zoo.

I was invited to lunch in a nearby rural home just off the main road by a gentle old lady and her vivacious daughter, who had produced spaghetti al sugo and watermelon, their

My hostess in her garden, Simeonovo

verandah table decked with dewy roses picked from their riotous garden. Next door they showed me greenhouses where neighbours grew blooms commercially. Octogenarian Mirka had never invited a foreign guest to her table before, but posed against her red roses with quiet pride. Ana, her unmarried daughter, busied herself in a Sofia shop all week, then relaxed at home at weekends, looking after the home and garden, and occasionally inviting over a friend.

'I have to look after my mother now she is old. I can't emigrate like some of the women I know. I could marry of course and stay here, but who would look after my mother, especially if I had children to think about? No, my dear, it's better like this. You know what makes me sad?'

'I can imagine, Ana, but tell me anyway.'

'What makes me sad is that a reporter came to me with a microphone and a camera the day after the fall of Zhivkov, and he told me that for the first time in my life I could say whatever I wanted to say. And you know, for the first time in my life I was so overcome with amazement that I couldn't say anything at all. For thirty years I had been storing up what I could say when such a thing happened to me, and yet I stood there silent as an idiot!'

Dozens of new private hotels are springing up in Simeonovo, once a village, but now a suburb. Among its attractions are clean air, the proximity to Vitosha for hikers and skiers, and a slower tempo compared with central Sofia. At the Delia Hotel, I found Dechko and Lilia Yordanov's comfortable villa modernised with new bathrooms and a bar in the basement. Lilia makes her own jam from wild strawberries, and bakes her own bread, which I took outside, among her scented pine-grove. At the Edelweiss Hotel I found the owner would provide you not only with bed and board, but also with horses for riding on Vitosha or cart-rides navigated by himself. The Kamenitsa, Bozhur and Korona Hotels looked equally well-patronised, but if you happen on a hotel without meals, you can try the excellent Panorama Restaurant in the centre of Simeonovo, specialised in tripe soup, roast lamb, and stuffed peppers.

АВТОБУСНИ ЛИНИИ ОТ АВТОГАР|

Автогара
Изток (20г)

с. Байлово	с. Пенкьовц
с. Богданлия	Перник
Ботевград	с. Рани луг
с. Бърдарски геран	Рилски м
с. Бъркач	Станке Д
Бухово	Трън
Велико Търново	с. Цигрилов
с. Габра	с. Чуковец*
Габрово	Якоруда
с. Гайтанево	
с. Гол. Раковица	**Автогара**
с. Гор. Богров	**Север (176**
с. Гор. Сливово	
с. Григорево	Белоград|
с. Дол. Богров	Берковиц|
с. Душанци	с. Брезе
Елин Пелин	с. Бяло пол|
Етрополе	Вършец
с. Желява	с. Гинци**
с. Йорданкино	Годеч
с. Каменица	с. Големо М
с. Катунец	с. Дълги де|
Козлодуй	Козлоду|
Копривщица	с. Мартинов|
с. Краево	Своге**
с. Лопян	
с. Лесидрен	**Автостанц|**
с. Литаково	**гара Захар|**
Ловеч	**фабрика (1**
Луковит	
Манаселска река	с. Алдомир|
с. Огняново	Банкя
с. Осоица	с. Божурищ|
Оряхово	с. Братушк|
с. Петрич	с. Бърложн|
с. Равно поле	с. Вишан
с. Рашково	с. Врабца
с. Своде	с. Гургулят
Севлиево	с. Златуша
Средногорие	с. Клисура
с. Стъргел	с. Пожарев|
с. Столник	с. Радулов|
Тетевен	с. Хераково|
ТМК Кремиковци	с. Храбърск|
Троян	с. Чеканец
Угърчин	
Хисар	**Автостанц|**
с. Чурек	**кв. Орланд|**
с. Яна	**(19а)** ·

Автогара
Юг (446)

	с. Войнягов|
	с. Кубратов|
Боровец	с. Локорско
Велинград	с. Негован
с. Говедарци	Нови Иск|
с. Клисура	с. Подгумер|
Мальовица	с. Световра|
Пазарджик	с. Чепинци
Панагюрище	
Самоков	**Автостанц|**
с. Сапарева баня	**жк Надежд|**
Смолян	
Стрелча	с. Балша
*с. Ярлово	с. Безден
	с. Богьовци

Автогара
Запад (40а)

	с. Божурище|
	с. Бучин про|
Банско	с. Василовц|
Благоевград	с. Волуяк
Бобов дол	с. Голяновц|
м. Бонсови поляни**	с. Градец
с. Бохова	с. Дробосла|
с. Голяма Фуча	с. Драговищ|
с. Горна Дикання	Костинбро|
Гоце Делчев	с. Мрамор
с. Дрен	с. Опицвет
с. Дълга лука	с. Петърч
с. Елешница	с. Понор
с. Завала*	Сливница
м. Златни мостове	с. Чибаовци
с. Кожинци	
м. Копитото	**Автостанц|**
Кюстендил	**жк Гео Мил|**
с. Лешниковци	**(33в)**
с. Лялинци	
	с. Герман

Map of Bus Routes throughout Greater Sofia

АД СОФИЯ

ЦИИ

с. Кокаляне
с. Лозен
с. Панчарево

Автостанция
гара Искър (36в)

с. Бусманци
с. Герман
с. Казичене
с. Кривина

Автостанция
жк Дървеница
(45в)

с. Бистрица
с. Железница
с. Плана

Автостанция
кв. Илиянци (6а)

с. Доброславци
с. Кътина
с. Мировяне
Нови Искър
(кв. Курило)
кв. Ал. Войков

Автостанция
кв. Княжево (38г)

с. Владая
с. Мърчаево
с. Рударци

Автостанция
Хладилника (42г)

хотел Морени
(Витоша)
с. Бистрица
с. Железница

Автостанция
жк Хр. Михайлов
(Западен парк) (28а)

с. Мало Бучино

Автостанция
жк Люлин 6 (14г)
Банка

◉ автогара
● автостанция в гр. София
○ автостанция извън град София
━━━ автобусна линия обслужваща
    област град София
━━━ областна граница
─── общинска граница
БАНКЯ име на община

Автобусна линия с прекъснат трафик

* сезонна (1.V-30.IX)
** само събота и неделя
*** само делник

36: VITOSHA AND THE MONASTIC LIFE

Hermits and monks seeking to evade the noise, bustle and secular trappings of city life have always escaped to the mountains. Bulgaria, so rich in forested mountains with fresh
water and abundant game, fish and fruit, has attracted such
contemplatives to isolated corners such as Rila and Rozhen,
Ivanovo and the hills around Turnovo (where beautiful Preobrazhenski Monastery recently fell victim to landslides).

Vitosha, Sofia's own wilderness, possessed so many mediaeval monasteries with a reputation for scholarship and
piety that it became known as 'little Athos'. There is a chair-
lift ('sedalkova vuzhena liniya' is the Bulgarian phrase) from
Dragalevski Monastery (near Vodenitsata Restaurant) up to
the Moreni Restaurant, or you can visit by car, bus or (for the
energetic hill-climber) on foot. As the monastery is now designated for use by nuns, and six are currently resident, the
only part of the ecclesiastical domain open to visitors is the
Church of the Assumption of the Virgin Mary, begun in the
reign of Tsar Ivan Alexander (1331-71) according to a charter
from Tsar Ivan Shishman (1371-93) now in the Zografski
Monastery library on Mount Athos. An inscription above the
church entrance reveals that its frescoes were contributed by
Radoslav Mavur of Sofia in 1476. Early in the 17th century
the nave frescoes were covered over with new paintings, possibly by Father Pimen, but if you look in the narthex you will
see the earlier work, including donor portraits of Radoslav,
his wife Vida, and their two sons. Other monasteries suffered
during the Ottoman period, but Dragalevski flourished, and
after 1382 was allowed to hold services, to train whiterobed
clergy (who may marry if they choose) and celibate black-
robed monks, and to worship the Christian God. It remained
a centre for monastic vocations, for icon-painting, and for its

Vitosha. Chair-lift from Dragalevtsi to Aleko

manuscripts, such as Nikola's Four Gospels (1469) now in the Hilendarski Monastery on Mount Athos; the so-called Dragalevski Four Gospels (1534) with a silver-plated cover made in 1648 by the Sofiote goldsmith Velko; and the celebrated Psaltery of 1598 copied by the brothers Danaïl, Stoyan and Vladko, now in the Athos Iverski monastery. Saints and ascetics on the exterior northern wall recall the age of hesychasts.

The perennial connection between secluded monasteries and liberation movements in Bulgaria is neatly illustrated here by the monk Gennadi's alliance with Vasil Levski, 'the Apostle of Freedom', who made the holy man a courier for Sofia's revolutionary movement. When the Turks captured the revolutionary Dimitur Obshti in 1872, menacing the rebels with collapse, Gennadi fled to Serbia and joined there Voivod Panayot Hitov. The secret committee in Sofia was reorganised in 1873 by Deacon Ignatius Rilski, who at the same time became abbot of Dragalevski. Liberation would not be long in coming. The interrelation of Church and State is perpetuated today because the Patriarch, whose advice is sought by successive Governments, has his official residence overshadowing the church, with suites of guest-rooms.

Dragalevtsi village lies between the villages of Simeonovo and Boyana, and like them is now incorporated into Greater Sofia, beyond the ring road on the foothills of Vitosha. Minor roads too, link these villages, and I took the minor road from Dragalevtsi to Boyana after taking a lunch of meat and kachamak (maize dough fried in a recipe created two hundred years ago) at the local restaurant in three modernised mills once powered by run-off mountain waters known hereabouts as the Dragalevska Reka or Dragalevtsi River.

During winter, fresh winds whirl round Vitosha and down to Sofia as it sparkles under a fresh fall of snow, to give a Londoner or New Yorker the feeling of having Ben Nevis or the Catskills within view: a wilderness above Whitehall or Wall Street. Much of Vitosha is in fact an official nature reserve, and in Boyana we find one of the nine official world heritage monuments of Bulgaria as nominated by Unesco. This is the sequence of three churches loosely called the Kaloyan Church, roughly contemporary with other mediaeval basilical churches without free-standing supports, and with developed arms arched to carry a dome, as in the case of Sveta Spasovitsa in Kyustendil or Sveti Petur & Paul in Nikopol.

The first church, dated to the late 10th or early 11th century, comprised a small cruciform space with a dome. It was enlarged in the 1250s by Sebastocrator Kaloyan, who is portrayed in carefully-restored frescoes with his wife Dessislava, not to be confused with Princess Maria Dessislava, the 14th-century heroine of Parashkev Hajiev's opera. Kaloyan added a rectangular lower storey as narthex and crypt, and an upper storey as a new church. The third epoch of this church dedicated to St Nicholas and the Holy Martyr Panteleimon represents the sturdy National Revival style of the mid-19th century which we associate with centres such as Koprivshtitsa, Tryavna, Melnik and Old Plovdiv.

The frescoes of 1259 depict 240 figures in 89 scenes, with fascinating realistic details, such as costumes and accessories of Bulgarian feudal life in scenes such as 'The Last Supper', where a typical check napkin lies on a table laden with food you might eat today: bread, garlic and radishes. The pictorial naturalism of the portraits heralds the beginning of a long tradition that will culminate in the Samokov School and Svetlin Rusev or Dechko Uzunov. Who could forget the steady gaze of bearded Kaloyan as donor, holding a model of the church, or Kaloyan's mild, gentle consort, or King Konstantin Asen with his queen Irina? In the southern room, a grizzled warrior saint stands with his firm spear across his golden halo. In the western room, watch how the sea boils and whirls below a ship carrying St Nicholas of Myra; how gracefully the chubby-faced boy Jesus confronts that animated throng of disputants in the Temple; how majestically in her regal robes Queen Helena (finder of the True Cross) transfixes your gaze. In the eastern room the manly figure of

Boyana Church. Queen Helena, a mural of 1259

St Eustratius gives us heart for the fight: we who look as earthly as he, understates the hagiographer, may by our own virtue and courage achieve an equal sanctity. How different is the Cimabue-like Crucifixion, where Christ's twisted body agonises white against a background dark with unspoken grief! How transcendently moving is the Harrowing of Hell, beyond space, beyond time, beyond words! Ethereally, Jesus absorbs and reflects concentrated stares from men and women of every age and every estate. A rare image of Christ Euergetes blesses us with a calm radiance found more commonly in Buddhist art. Whether you prefer the sixteen scenes from the life of St Nicholas or the sensitive, loving individuality of contemporary portraits, Boyana will always remain with you as a treasury of 13th-century art fully equal to the glories of Turnovo. And recall as you breathe in the pure mountain air that this church led directly into the Sebastocrator's palace within a fortress complex, with large kitchens, stables, and more than one aristocratic residence. A ruined tower on Maiden's Rock (Momina Skala) is evidence of a watchtower to secure the fortress; archaeologists have uncovered traces of waterpipes which assured year-round water-supply against the possibility of siege. Nowadays a cabin-lift from Knyazhevo up to Kopitoto will bring you to Kopitoto hotel-restaurant with stunning views over Sofia; if the cabin-lift isn't working, take bus 62.

Another cabin-lift gives access from Simeonovo up to the levels of three hotel-restaurants: Shtastlivetsa, the biggest on Vitosha, the slightly smaller Prostor, and the tiny Moreni, where I enjoyed an outstandingly good lunch overlooking snow-covered Sofia. Skiing equipment is available on hire locally; tuition can be found very cheaply. Aleko Ski Centre caters to 35,000 visitors a day on average, most of them Bulgarians. In summer a serviceable road leads up to Cherni Vruh (Black Peak), at 2290 metres the highest peak on Vitosha.

Passing across to Western Vitosha, you come to the locality of Zlatni Mostove (Golden Bridges), with its own restaurants.

Whether you like hiking, skiing, or merely driving in the mountains, Vitosha provides an ever-changing amenity of fresh air and colour throughout the year.

It was in a Vitosha villa that a poet-friend of mine prominent during the Zhivkov era was pressed about his political views, never publicly avowed. 'I always had certain opinions', he readily admitted to the assembled circle. 'The difference is, now I agree with them.'

37: BANKYA

You can get to Bankya by bus, but I prefer the little train that commutes every 30 minutes morning and afternoon between Sofia Central Station and Bankya. The ticket office, as for all 'local' stations such as Mezdra, is downstairs at Sofia Central and there are always patient queues, but if you miss one train there's always another to the self-proclaimed 'gradut na zdraveto': the town of health. Turn right out of Bankya station and the information booth on Ulitsa Tsar Osvoboditel provides maps and accommodation information from 8 a.m. to 8 p.m. seven days a week. Hotels are located at Ropotamo 16, Stamboliiski 50 and Stamboliiski 90, but more spring up as families in lovely old patrician houses modernise rooms for guests.

Though only ten miles from the capital, Bankya's woods and hills seem as far from city apartment blocks as Vermont autumn colours from Manhattan's congestion. The town grew around a spa for treating gastro-intestinal disorders, nervous diseases, and heart conditions. The waters average 36.5°C (98°F). Treatment is available in a polyclinic and there are sporting facilities such as tennis courts and a fine open-air swimming pool. Its healthy climate and quiet wooded hills appealed to Todor Zhivkov, who built a luxurious mansion with sentry-boxes for security, his own swimming pool, sauna rooms and fifty medical cubicles. Zhivkov's palace, with marble floors and wooden panelled ceilings, was designed by Nikola Nikolov (1972-4) as a government balneological centre, but President Zhivkov liked it so much that he kept it for his own private use. After the coup of 10 November 1989, the new government stated an intention to convert it for use as a hospital for sick children, but they later asserted that 'it was unsuitable' for that purpose, and Sofia City Council

Bankya. Health resort

turned it over to the wealthy Japanese balletomane Masako Ohya and it is now known above the door as her 'Country Club'. A public relations lady claimed 90% occupancy of the 8 rooms and nine suites, including an opulent presidential suite. A room without any meals costs 150 leva for Bulgarians (800 leva for foreigners) and a suite costs 250 leva for Bulgarians (2,000 leva for foreigners). I chatted to the former lifeguard in the heated indoor swimming pool. 'It was a good job,' he confessed sheepishly. 'I had to look after just one man, maybe once a day, some weeks, maybe half-an-hour at a time. And he was a good swimmer!'

The dissident Todor Kolev, having daringly derided the Zhivkov regime in a Chaplinesque guise, tells a story about postage stamps. Zhivkov heard that stamps with his portrait were selling in small numbers compared with other kinds of stamps. He went into a post office incognito and asked what the matter was. The assistant shrugged and said, 'It seems that the ones with your face don't stick.' Zhivkov was puzzled, so he bought one, spat on the back and it stuck down on the counter perfectly. 'What's the problem?' he demanded.

'Ah', nodded the assistant, 'that's what they're doing wrong. Everyone else is spitting on the front.'

'Nowadays we get here mainly wealthy Japanese, Italians, Swiss, Greeks, and Germans. Some apartments are leased for three months on special discount.'

Bankya. The former residence of President Todor Zhivkov, now the Masako Ohya Country Club

175

Beautifully landscaped, the luxurious country club with its camouflaged sentry boxes seems like a defensive palace of comfort distanced from a city where Stefan Ninov of Sofia City People's Council in 1988 told me 315,024 new flats had been built in 30 years, and 20,000 more were planned for each year of the current five-year plan. Capitalist societies frankly acknowledge the existence of inequalities between council-housing and royal palaces; communist societies were unable to justify differential treatment, so hypocritically pretended they didn't exist. Vrani, Arbanasi, Rusalka, Bankya: these are just a few of the palatial homes of the nomenklatura, the party faithful.

I strolled back down Ulitsa Slivnitsa to the town centre, then saw an open-air service under way before a church on a hill. I climbed there in time for a ceremony mirroring hundreds of others throughout Bulgaria that day. It was 22 September, anniversary eve of the execution in 1947 by the communists of Nikola Petkov, leader of the Agrarian Party. A wrinkled old man in brown wiped his eyes as he recalled those black days in 1947. Everything had seemed so hopeful in February, when the Paris treaty seemed to guarantee complete equality and full civil rights for all Bulgarian citizens, and required all Soviet troops to leave Bulgaria within ninety days. The anti-communist opposition in Parliament demanded a ban on the Communist Party as one the fascist organisations banned under the treaty, and Petkov demanded to know from Georgi Dimitrov why expenditure on prisons and the police had quintupled in five years. Dimitrov then caused Petkov to be arrested in the Parliament building itself, presumably *pour encourager les autres,* forbade him a defence lawyer to overturn the trumped-up charges, imported peasants from the countryside to demand Petkov's death as a traitor, and hanged him like a criminal without the last sacraments or religious burial.

Here on this hill we commemorated the heroic democrat and libertarian Petkov, whose murder caused a deep and permanent split in his Agrarian Party, between those who

176

claimed that he and he alone stood for independent agrarian principles and those fellow-travellers who sought privilege and power within the newly monolithic one-party state. The priest intoned prayers for the soul of Petkov in that intense, urgent, melodious Church Slavonic bass which seems to emerge from the Middle Ages. If you close your eyes you can picture it in the mouths of the apostles Cyril and Methodius as they stand forever strong and united in front of Sofia's National Library.

Sunlight slanted through the dense trees above Bankya. The solemn crowd, many in tears now, clutched flowers, lit candles, clasped each other's hands, bowed heads, and in their Sunday best shrieked silently by their very presence here at their past Communist oppressors. We are here, defied that semi-circle, to identify ourselves as the victims. We denounce nobody, we scream at nobody, but here we stand, as if to fulfil decades of unwritten promises, to testify against the lies of Georgi Dimitrov. Within, the little dark church glowed with candles. Light flowed in through a window beyond the iconostasis, whose gleaming polished wood poured its own lustre on the crucifixion framed by the window; above the crucifixion a stylised Last Supper centred on the haloed Christ. One does not have to have been born and bred into the Orthodox Church to stand transfixed at such moments by the still beauty of silence on a hallowed hill.

Through the town I meandered, eventually on Ulitsa Kiril i Metodi coming across a crowded café: always a good sign. A waitress came and asked what I should like. 'What have you got?' 'Kiselo mlyako i banitsa' – yoghourt and flaky pastry with cream cheese. Jars of locally-grown honey sat invitingly on a stall nearby so I bought one of those, scooped a spoonful into my excellent yoghourt, and passed the jar round to the family who had just sat at my table.

'Ivailo', announced the paterfamilias, pumping my hand. His plump wife looked as though she had fed well for forty-five years and today would be no exception.

'England?' pondered Ivailo between mouthfuls of banitsa,

Bankya. Selling honey outside a restaurant

'is good. I have seen factories in England, modern machinery, exact punctuality, measuring carefully, cold in human relations, analytical, calculating, you have fine mathematicians, Babbage, Darwin, Rutherford...'

'Well, actually Rutherford was...'

'What I call a mature society, not like children. We Slavs', he pointed to both his chins and all three of his wife's, 'are still adolescent, what you call 'natural' like springs gushing out at Bankya, we say what we want without thinking, thoughtless, hot people, we have great opera singers, Kabaivanska, Ghiaurov.'

'Do you think it might be better to combine the best features of both?'

'You mean, Bulgarians to marry English people?'

'Perhaps you needn't take it so far. Just adopt some of the better characteristics from both temperaments.'

'You can't reconcile such different temperaments. If you don't agree with a man in Bulgaria, you shout at him, put him in jail, ban him, deport him, burn his writings...'

'Maybe now things will be different. After all, you can say what you like.'

'That's what I mean. Englishmen always take a balanced position, see the opposition point of view. If you don't agree with someone you give him his own political party, his own newspaper, his own Hyde Park what is crate of *sapun*?'

'His soapbox.'

'You want to hear many opinions. That is the way of consensus, like in Japan. You have strong opposition, stopping the Government from abusing power. That is good.'

'Here's a toast to strong opposition.'

'English is good', he said, literally slapping his thigh as he winked at me. 'But Germany is better. Next month we emigrate!'

USEFUL INFORMATION

When to Come

Most visitors to Bulgaria come to the Black Sea in the summer and the mountains for skiing in the winter, and even if you intend to spend most of your time in Sofia, it may be worth looking at such packages, which may cost less than the flight only on a regular scheduled flight to Sofia, if you bear in mind that internal flights, buses or trains are all extremely cheap by Western standards. You can then use your booked hotel room on the first and last night at no charge. At peak times, accommodation may become a problem unless you book ahead, but a recent decline in tourism throughout Eastern Europe has greatly improved your chances in that regard. Remember that Sofia's Vitosha mountain is itself a skiing resort, so you can combine city pleasures in the evening with winter sports by day. Early December through February is the best time, though up-to-date weather reports can be obtained from your local travel agent.

Hiking on Vitosha is wonderful throughout the rest of the year, too. Sofia is perhaps at its best (though Sofiotes are by no means agreed on this) in May and September, but the weather is generally mild throughout the year, avoiding the summer heat found on coastal plains as well as the winter freezing found on the Stara Planina ridges, often cut off by blizzards in January.

The number one tour operator from Britain to Bulgaria is Balkan Holidays, 19 Conduit St., London W1R 9TD; from Ireland, Balkan Tours, 5-6 South Great George's St., Dublin and 9-10 Lombard St., Belfast BT1 1RB. Your travel agent will be able to recommend other tour operators, including Ingham's and Intasun, Phoenix and Global, Sunquest and Peltours,

Trafalgar and Cosmos. Many new Bulgarian private tour operators will design visits around your requirements once you arrive in Sofia.

How to Come

Most charter flights to Bulgaria arrive in the summer months at Burgas and Varna for Black Sea resorts. For Sofia, check availability at your local travel agent, unless you intend to obtain a package.

Sofia Airport, situated very close to the city centre, is best reached by the cheap frequent buses 84 (normal) and 284 (express). Taxis come much dearer. A few taxi-drivers are unwilling to use meters when driving foreigners, and may harass you to change money on the black market, an offer to avoid at all costs. Balkan Airlines have offices at 12 Ploshtad Narodno Subranie (near Grand Hotel Sofia), 19 Ulitsa Lege, and 10 Ul. Sofiiska Komuna. Flights to Sofia take 23 hours from Tokyo, 14 hours from New York, 3 hours from London or Paris, and 1½ hours from Vienna. Other European capitals currently offering direct flights include Berlin, Amsterdam, Brussels, Madrid, Copenhagen and Rome.

By rail, Sofia is connected with Moscow by daily departures via Pleven, Ruse, Bucharest and Kiev; with Warsaw and Berlin (via Budapest and Prague); with Istanbul, Thessaloniki and Athens, and with Ljubljana, capital of Slovenia. There is a first-rate domestic rail service, and while staying in Sofia you should try to make time for the spectacular rail trip along the Iskur Gorge to Mezdra. Bus routes serving the Central Station are 74, 77, 85, 213, 285, and 313. Tram routes are 1, 6, 7, 8, 9, 12 and 15. To reserve international rail tickets, you have a choice of Wagons-Lits at 10 Ul. Lege (tel. 87 34 52) or Rila at 5 Ul. Gurko (tel. 87 07 77). To buy domestic rail tickets in advance, try the ticket centre at the National Palace of Culture, now called Sofia Congress Centre (59 31 06), or offices at 23 Dimitrov Bulevard (87 02 22) or 8 Ploshtad Slaveikov (87 57 42).

Buses are just as cheap, frequent and reliable as trains

serving Sofia. The international bus terminal at 23 Bul. Mihailov serves Yugoslav and Greek destinations. Domestic bus terminals are located on Ulitsa 9 Septemvri (West Terminal) for Rila Monastery; on Ploshtad Pirdop (North Terminal, to the terminus of tram 3 then a five-minute walk) for Northern Bulgaria; the East Terminal (tram 14 from Sveta Nedelya) for Plovdiv.

By road, the E-80 crosses Europe from La Coruña, Toulouse, Nice, Genoa, Rome and Dubrovnik, continuing to Edirne and Istanbul; the E-70 from La Rochelle and Lyon passes Turin, Verona, Trieste, Zagreb, Belgrade and Bucharest to end up in Ruse and Varna; and the E-79 crosses Romania from Oradea and Craiova, touching Vidin and Botevgrad before continuing to Thessaloniki.

Driving in Bulgaria is pleasant on three counts: you can go where your fancy leads you; the roads are emptier than in Western Europe; and because of the total ban on drinking any quantity of alcohol no matter how small, the roads are relatively safe. Driving is on the right.

The speed limit is 120 kph on motorways, 80 kph on other roads outside built-up areas, and 60 kph in built-up areas unless signs are posted to the contrary. You will want to learn the Cyrillic alphabet if only for the road signs. Petrol coupons may be bought at the borders, at Balkantourist hotels and motels, and at some travel agencies overseas. You may drive on your current national licence as long as you can prove insurance cover for third-party liability, and show Green and Blue cards, the latter being available at border checkpoints. If you belong to a motoring organisation affiliated with A.I.T. or F.I.A., the Shipka Travel Agency provides free road aid on breakdowns requiring an hour's work or less, and repatriation of damaged vehicles. Costs of labour are much lower than in Western Europe.

You can drive your own car, but the journey through Europe is very long compared with the size of Bulgaria and my advice is to hire a self-drive car (limited or unlimited mileage as you prefer) at the airports of Sofia, Burgas or Varna; at the Grand Hotel Sofia or Vitosha-New Otani in Sofia; at the Novotel in Plovdiv; or at the Black Sea in the major hotels in Sunny Beach (Slunchev Bryag), Burgas, Golden Sands (Zlatni Pyasutsi), Albena, Druzhba and Varna. Otherwise you will not have easy access to monasteries and museumtowns off the beaten track.

Taxis are plentiful and can be hailed in the street, hired by phone, or awaited in a taxi-rank. The charges are very low and most drivers exceptionally honest: they do not expect to be tipped.

Accommodation
The Interhotel chain in Bulgaria operates five hotels in Sofia: the five-star Hotel Vitosha-New Otani outside the centre at 100 Bulevard Ivanov and Sheraton-Balkan at 1 Sveta Nedelya Square in the city-centre; the four-star Novotel Evropa at 131 Dimitrov Bulevard very convenient for the Central Rail Station; and the three-star Park Hotel Moskva at 25 Ulitsa Nezabravka, at the southern perimeter of Park na Svobodata (Freedom Park), and Grand Hotel Sofia, off Bulevard Ruski, facing the Parliament building.

Other hotels include the four-star businessmen's hotel favoured by Arabs, the Rodina at 8 Bul. General Totleben; the three-star Hemus at 31 Bulevard Traikov on the way from the National Palace of Culture up to Vitosha; and the Bulgaria, 4 Bulevard Ruski near the National Art Gallery; and several two-star establishments: the Serdika near the Levski Monument and Makedonski Music Theatre; the Slavia at 2 Ul. Sofiiski Geroi; and Slavianska Beseda at 127 Ulitsa Rakovski, in the theatre and gallery district. Hotel Pliska is the nearest overnight stop for the airport. If you have plenty of time and prefer walking in the mountains to city pleasures, four hotels on Mount Vitosha are worth considering. Kopitoto (tel. 57 12 96) stands above Knyazhevo, accessible from the centre by tram 5, followed by bus 62. In a different area of the mountain, you have the choice of the three-star Prostor (tel. 65 48 81), or the two-star Moreni (tel. 65 29 69) and Shtastlivetsa (tel. 66 50 24) both accessible by chairlift from Dragalevtsi or by tram 2 from Ulitsa Graf Ignatiev, followed by bus 66. Vitosha is becoming a paradise for seekers of private villas, apartments or rooms, as home-owners supplement their income. When roaming for such deals, you can be assured that you will be treated royally, even if you are staying only a few days.

Motoring in Bulgaria will become much more popular as the excellent public transport inevitably leaps in cost to businesslike levels which permit necessary reinvestment. At the moment, trains, buses, trolleybuses and trams are not being maintained or replaced, which will lead to a crisis. Bulgarians have been brought up to believe that transport should be so cheap as to be virtually free, and if the market economy ever arrives, it will bring a shock to those who currently refuse to pay for a tram ticket because it is to expensive.

Motels and roadside tourist complexes do exist, but many more will be needed in the near future to cope with the expected influx of international tourism. At present, three three-star complexes can be found on the E80 international highway: Iztok (East) 12 km from Sofia, Bozhur 27 km from Sofia, and Ihtiman 50 km from Sofia. Of the three two-star motels, one is in Boyana, near the famous Boyana Church; another also on Mount Vitosha: the Tihiya Kut, 12 km from the centre; and the last in the suburb of Gorublyane on the E80 highway to Plovdiv, past the turn to the airport. Also near Gorublyane is the Vrana Campsite, 10 km from the centre and close to the Ring Road (southeast). The other campsite, 11 km from the centre on the E79 highway, is the Cherniya Kos, or Blackbird, also designated with two stars.

But by far the best and cheapest way to get to know Sofia and its fascinating people is to live with them as a paying guest, which is easily accomplished by making for the Balkantourist Private Lodgings office at Bul. Dondukov 37 near the Largo (tel. 88 06 55, telex 22488). You will pay in advance for the number of nights you require, a period which may of course be extended by local agreement. By paying a few extra leva a day I enjoyed the use of the kitchen, as well as all bathroom facilities, and became firm friends with the family in a matter of hours. This is undoubtedly the way to live in Sofia, unless you prefer to live outside in a suburban guest-house, such as in Simeonovo, as described in the text. As I go to press, the immigration authorities have still not waived the totalitarian rule requiring foreigners to declare where they spend every night of their stay, which means that theoretically you should not accept offers of private accommodation made on arrival at the airport, Central Rail Station or bus stations, because such unofficial accommodation will not be authorised to stamp your visa. In practice, immigration officials no longer see any cause to scrutinise your visa for evidence of illicit nights unaccounted for. They are much more likely to wish you a pleasant journey, and thank you for visiting Bulgaria.

Restaurants
On a package tour all your meals will be carefully planned in advance. The first shock will be the price, which will come to about 10% of what you would expect to pay in Europe or the U.S.A., equivalent to a tip in your usual restaurant. The second shock will be that by no means all the items on the most extensive menu will be available, and it is best to ask the waiter. Since the spread of private cafés and restaurants, there is a wider choice but prices are rising all the time.

Breakfast will usually be a cold buffet, but if you prefer something hot, an egg dish will often emerge on demand: 'hamniks' being recognised as 'ham and eggs'; an omelette with cheese or tomato even more commonly available. You will expect fruit juice, cereal and milk, two or three types of cheese and cold meats, yoghourt of prime quality, white bread (why never any brown?) with jam or honey and butter, tea and coffee. Lunch and dinner will start with salad or soup, and a small range of dishes stressing lamb, pork and veal, with only rarely fish and the occasional chicken. Dessert will consist of fruit, ice-cream, cake or crème caramel where available, but most city restaurants except those in hotels expect clients to take dessert at a café or *sladkarnitsa* (ice-cream shop). Service will often be dreadfully slow, because few (except the top hotels) have enough waiters and because Bulgarians traditionally spend a long time over meals, treating them as social occasions for good conversation.

In Sofia you should try the Forum Restaurant (no. 64) and the Havana (no. 27) on Bulevard Vitosha, the Rubin on Sveta Nedelya Square, the Kristal at 10 Ul. Aksakov; for German food the Berlin (no. 2) and for Polish food the Warszawa (no. 15) on Bulevard Zaimov; for Korean food the Pyongyang at 24 Ul. Zlatarov; for very expensive Japanese food the Vitosha-New Otani at 100 Bulevard Ivanov; for Hungarian food (with intrusive 'gipsy' violins) the Budapest at 145 Ul. Rakovski; and for Vietnamese cuisine the Vietnam at 1 Bulevard Kirkov.

Folk-style restaurants often present folkdancing in the evenings and again should not be relied on for quick service if you have appointments after dinner. It is quite usual to dine *after* opera or theatre performances which invariably begin at 7 p.m., but normally last orders cannot be placed after 11 p.m. at *mehani*, equivalent to Greek *tavernas*, such as Shumako (bus 98 to Simeonovo), Vodenitsata or Vodenicharski Mehani (bus 93 to Dragalevtsi) and the popular Boyansko Hanche (bus 63 to Boyana). Bulgarian cuisine of this type is available at many places in Sofia, such as the Bulgarska Gozba (no. 34) and Rozhen (no. 74) on Vitosha Bulevard, Tetevenska Sreshta at 125 Rakovski, or Pod Lipite (1 Ul. Elin Pelin).

Because I don't like spending three hours over a meal while in Sofia, I tend to take bigger meals in central self-service restaurants, though the food is not very appetising, and snacks while walking along, a common sight in all Bulgarian towns. Enterprising men will set up hot-dog stalls, scarfed women preside over bags of popcorn, side-windows open from restaurants to serve delicious take-aways such as a *banitsa* or open sandwiches with cheese and salami; fruit-stalls offer rare delicacies such as a bunch of bananas or a box of oranges. The rule is always 'buy it when you see it, because you may never see it again'. Try food shops (*hranitelni stoki, gastronom,* or *magazin*) because their prices will always be well below what you would pay at home, and they will help to vary your diet in Sofia. And of course if you like wine don't forget to take some back home, for its quality is as high as its cost is low, like the cognac and the apricot brandy.

Passports and Visas
You must be in possession of a full passport, but package-tourists do not require a separate visa each at the time of writing: it is however advisable to check the current position with your local travel agent, or the Bulgarian National Tourist Offices abroad, (in the U.K.) at 18 Princes St., London W1R 7RE; in the U.S. at 161 E. 86th St., New York, N.Y. 10028; and in Canada c/o Bulgarian Trade Mission, 1550 De Maisonneuve West, Montréal, Quebec. In the Netherlands, the address is 43 Leidsestraat, 1017 NV Amsterdam; in Germany you could try 1-3 Stefanstrasse, 6000 Frankfurt/Main 1 or 175 Kurfürstendamm, 1000 Berlin 15; in France the address is 45 Avenue de l'Opéra, 75002 Paris, and in Belgium it is 62 Rue Ravenstein, 1000 Brussels. It is worth stressing that anyone planning *individual* tourism, including individual deviations within package tours, must have a visa at present, and must have a rubber stamp from the hotel reception at both arrival and departure there, failing which a fine may be levied on leaving the country.

Apply for longer than you need in case of delays (the fee will be the same), and allow at least three weeks before departure.

Customs and Currency
You may neither import nor export Bulgarian leva, and you should keep receipts for hard currency changed into leva so that you can change back (into a currency that may not be

what you prefer) at the point of departure. Allow time for this. There are 100 stotinki (100 means 'sto') in a lev and at present the highest denomination of notes is 20 leva. Always double-check, because these matters have a way of changing overnight, but at present there are three official rates of exchange: the base rate subject to weekly review, the 100% premium available at all Balkantourist offices and hotels, and a premium rate far above this which I found in banks and major department stores such as the Sofia Central Universal Supermarket (TsUM). I exchanged sterling travellers' cheques for leva while in Bulgaria, and was offered either US dollars or Deutschmarks on leaving, when I produced my receipts. A vigorous black market exists, but I urge you not to be tempted into illegal deals, no matter how attractive the offer. Quite apart from the criminal offence involved, the cost of living is already so low in Bulgaria that there can be little if any good cause to risk your liberty for a few extra leva.

Customs searches are not likely to worry the foreign tourist. You may bring in and take out at the moment 250 cigarettes, 2 litres of wine and 1 litre of spirits. On entry, declare radios, tape recorders, TV sets, cameras and typewriters; on departure, declare gifts and purchases totalling in excess of 50 leva – the only question customs officers asked me was 'Have you any leva?'. There is no restriction on the import or export of any hard currency.

Electricity
Sofia's power is 220-240 volts, 50 cycles, A.C. Winter cuts are common, due to overloading of the system and to irregular supplies. Take candles for your own use in hotels, and matches; I always pack a torch for emergencies.

Embassies
Britons and Commonwealth citizens use the British Embassy at 65 Bulevard Tolbuhin (tel. 88-53-61 and 87-83-25), except that Canadians use the U.S. Embassy at 1 Bulevard Stamboliiski (tel. 88-48-01, -02, and -03). The Belgian Embassy is at

19 Frédéric Joliot-Curie St., ap. 6 and 8; the Netherlands at 19a Denkoglu St., the French at 29 Oborishte Bulevard, and the German at 7 Henri Barbusse St.

Health
In Sofia the Clinic for Foreigners can be found at Mladost 1, 1 Evgeni Pavlovski St. (tel. 75 361), and the main hotels have a doctor on call. No charge is made for consultation and treatment in emergencies; longer treatment will be charged for (always reasonably) if Bulgaria does not have a reciprocal agreement with the Government of the country to which the patient belongs.

Office Hours
Due to the necessity of taking a second job, some Bulgarians may not attend at office hours as advertised, between 8-5 or 9-5 with a fairly extended lunch hour for shopping. This should not be a matter for criticism on the part of foreigners whose lifestyle may be more comfortable and affluent.

Speaking (and Reading) the Language
Bulgarian is very close to Serbo-Croat, the main language of Yugoslavia, though it has affinities with all the other Slavonic languages. Closely akin to Russian, it shares the Cyrillic alphabet (with a few minor differences) and if you prefer not to spend time learning the language, rest assured that a knowledge of the alphabet alone will take you a long way in Bulgaria. You will recognise at once, for example, 'telefon', 'muzei', 'hotel', 'galeria', 'kino', 'teatur', 'petrol' and of course the names of cities, towns and villages on road-signs, maps and leaflets. I have transliterated Cyrillic consistently for the most part, though 'Sofiya' is given its traditional Italianate form. The soft sign when a vowel is shown as 'u' in 'Turnovo', on the analogy of 'Bulgaria', and when a consonant as 'y', the pronunciation of 'Kolyo Ficheto', the self-taught master-builder.

BULGARIAN ALPHABET

А а	a	К к	k	Ф ф	f
Б б	b	Л л	l	Х х	h
В в	v	М м	m	Ц ц	ts
Г г	g	Н н	n	Ч ч	ch
Д д	d	О о	o	Ш ш	sh
Е е	e	П п	p	Щ щ	sht
Ж ж	zh	Р р	r	Ъ ъ	a, u
З з	z	С с	s	Ь ь	
И и	i	Т т	t	Ю ю	yu
Й й	y	У у	u	Я я	ya

Few textbooks exist, and the only dictionaries I have found had to be hunted down in a dozen bookshops because they sell out so quickly. The *English-Bulgarian Dictionary* (2 vols., 1987) by Maria Rankova and others is published by the Nauka i Izkustvo Publishing House, Sofia, who also issue one-volume *Bulgarian-English* and *Bulgarian-French* dictionaries. In the absence of a teach-yourself style grammar with a key to exercises, the only convenient grammar is *A Course in Modern Bulgarian* (2nd ed., 2 vols., 1983) by Milka Hubenova and others, from Slavica Publishers, Inc., P.O. Box 14388, Columbus, Ohio 43214. To learn Bulgarian through the literature, you might like to know that Sofia Press has produced a multilingual version of Hristo Botev's *Immortality* (1988), and the great historical novel by the national poet Ivan Vazov, *Pod Igoto* (10th impression, 1988), can be studied side-by-side with the English translation, *Under the Yoke* and the French version *Sous le Joug* (both Sofia Press).

Russian was the commonest foreign language taught in Bulgaria, but is now being overtaken by English, French and German.

Words and Phrases
Good morning (first thing)   Dobro utro
Good day (until evening)   Dobur den

191

Good evening	Dobur vecher
Goodnight	Leka nosht
Yes, no	Da, ne
Please tell me...	Molya, kazhete mi...
Thank you	Merci *or* blagodarya
What is the time?	Kolko e chasut?
Do you speak English?	Govorite li angliiski?
I don't understand you	Ne vi razbiram
Excuse me	Izvinete
Where is Solunska Street?	Kude se namira Ulitsa Solunska?
Straight on	Na pravo
Here, there	Tuk, tam
To the left	V lyavo
To the right	V dyasno
How much do I owe?	Kolko tryabva da platya?
Speak more slowly	Govorite po bavno
Goodbye	Dovizhdane
I wish to exchange money	Iskam da obmenya pari
How far is it to Plovdiv?	Kolko e daleche do Plovdiv?
A first-class ticket to Varna	Edin bilet purva klasa za Varna
When does the train leave for Gabrovo?	Koga trugva vlakut za Gabrovo?
Please, help me!	Molya, pomognete mi!
A single room, with bath	Edna staya s edno leglo sus banya
Toilet	Toaleta (M for men; Zh for women)
Entrance; exit	Vhod; izhod
How much does it cost?	Kolko struva?
What is this called?	Kak se kazva tova?
Open, closed	Otvoren, zatvoren
No smoking	Pusheneto zabraneno
Under repair	Na remont
Vacant, occupied	Svoboden, zaet
Today, tomorrow	Dnes, utre

Numbers and Days of the Week
1 edin, edna, edno 2 dva, dve 3 tri 4 chetiri 5 pet 6 shest 7
sedem 8 osem 9 devet 10 deset 11 edinadeset 12 dvanadeset
13 trinadeset 14 chetirinadeset 15 petnadeset 16 shest-
nadeset 17 sedemnadeset 18 osemnadeset 19 devetnadeset
(from 11 to 19 'nadeset' is often contracted to 'naiset') 20
dvadeset 21 dvadeset i edno 30 trideset 40 chetirideset 50
petdeset 60 shestdeset 70 sedemdeset 80 osemdeset 90 devet-
deset 100 sto 120 sto i dvadeset 200 dvesta 500 petstotin
1,000 hiliada 1st purvi purva purvo 2nd vtori vtora vtoro 3rd
treti treta treto

Monday	ponedelnik	Friday	petuk
Tuesday	vtornik	Saturday	subota
Wednesday	sryada	Sunday	nedelya
Thursday	chetvurtuk		

Months and Seasons

January	yanuari	Winter	zima
February	fevruari		
March	mart		
April	april	Spring	prolet
May	mai		
June	yuni	Summer	lyato
July	yuli		
August	avgust		
September	septemvri	Autumn	esen
October	oktomvri		
November	noemvri		
December	dekemvri	Christmas	koleda

Holidays and Festivals

January 1	New Year's Day
February	New Bulgarian Music, Sofia
	Throughout Bulgaria, Wine Growers' Day
	on the 14th

May 1-2	International Labour Day
May 24	Day of Bulgarian Culture and the Slavonic Alphabet
June	International Book Fair in Sofia (even years)
September 9-10	Socialist Revolution Day (this may be removed from the official calendar)
November 7	Great October Revolution Day (this may soon be removed from the calendar)
	Jazz weeks, Sofia
December	Musical Evenings, Sofia.

Telephones

Local calls within Sofia (and within any other city in Bulgaria) can be made from the abundant kiosks mounted on walls. You can speak as long as you desire for the initial coin (currently 2 stotinki, or less than 1 U.S. cent) and you should confirm meetings or appointments beforehand. Don't arrive at private homes unannounced.

Time

Sofia is one hour ahead of Central European Time, two hours ahead of Greenwich Mean Time in winter and three hours ahead of G.M.T. in summer, and seven hours ahead of Eastern Standard Time, U.S.A. Local 'summer time' applies from early April to late September.

Toilets

Most toilets have a charge currently varying between 30 and 50 stotinki. If you have no change, the attendant will give it to you, but never leave without paying because that is probably the attendant's only source of income.

Things to Remember

Bring your own camera equipment and enough films; very few foreign-language newspapers and magazines are obtainable in Bulgaria; a nod of the Bulgarian head usually means

194

'no' and a shake 'yes', but the opposite is not unknown, so beware! To dial 'fire' in Sofia, the number is 160; 'ambulance' is 150; and road aid from the Union of Bulgarian Motorists 146. Electricity is 220 volts. Museums are usually closed on Mondays; on other days they could be open from 8 to 6 or 6.30 in summer, closing earlier in winter, and some close for lunch. Shops close on Sundays; on other days they are usually open from 9-1 and 2-7.30. Laundrettes and dry cleaning services are very rare, but you can get laundry done (well and cheaply) at all major hotels. Large rail stations have twenty-four-hour left-luggage offices marked 'garderob', to adapt the French term. If self-catering, pack your own favourite brands of tea or coffee, which will be unobtainable in Bulgaria, like brown sugar or artificial sweeteners.

To join the British-Bulgarian Friendship Society, write to the Secretary, c/o Finsbury Library, 245 St. John St., London EC1V 4NB. As well as films, parties, lectures, and opportunities to meet Bulgarians on exchange visits, the Society organises general and special-interest tours with full board that often cost less than the return flight London-Sofia-London. Typical tours in any given year might emphasise birds, wine, art and architecture, education, medical treatment, textiles and embroidery, folk-dancing, and music.

Books and Maps

My favourite history of Bulgaria is Crampton's *A Short History of Modern Bulgaria* (Cambridge, 1987), but this could be supplemented on the archaeological side by D.M. Lang's *The Bulgarians from pagan times to the Ottoman Conquest* (London, 1976) and Mercia Macdermott's *A History of Bulgaria, 1393-1885* (London, 1962); the latter enjoys cult-heroine status in Bulgaria for her sympathetic biographies of Vasil Levski, Gotse Delchev, and Yane Sandanski. My favourite Bulgarian travel book is by Ivan Vazov: *The Great Rila Wilderness* (Sofia, 1969), incorporating also his essays 'In the Heart of the Rhodope Mountains' and 'A Recess of Stara

Planina', on a walk up to the Promised Rock not far from Sopot. My own *Bulgaria: a Travel Guide (1989)* is published by the Oleander Press of Cambridge worldwide except for the U.S.A. (Pelican Publishing Company, 1991), and the Oleander Press have also published my selection of ninety-two monologues entitled *Bulgarian Voices: Letting the People Speak* (1992).

For up-to-date brochures and maps, your local Bulgarian National Tourist Office will provide a selection, though the current free *Motoring across Bulgaria* (printed in English) reflects the 1983 *Putna Karta* ('Road map') in Cyrillic letters which has merely been reprinted, and hence does not include the major new international freeways crossing the country. Hiking maps of mountain regions are published by the Bulgarian Tourist Union, 30 Stamboliiski Bulevard, Sofia 1000.

Town plans can sometimes be found in kiosks or bookshops or stationery stores, but if all else fails a basic town plan of Sofia (large and small scale), can be found on the other side of the *Putna Karta* (again, only in Cyrillic).

INDEX

38, 46, 48, 125, 168, 177
Bulgarian Philatelists' Union
159
Bulgarian Red Cross 70
Bulgarian Socialist Party 10,
18-22, 26, 36, 91-2
Bulgarian Tourist Union 196
Bulgarska Gozba Restaurant
187
Burbanov, P. 80
Burgas 124
burials 65
buses 1, 6-7, 182-3
Büyük Cami 31, 42-5
Byzantium and the
Byzantines 27-32, 165

cabin lifts 171
cafés 9
capital status 58
cars and driving 183-4
Catholics 48
cats 110
censorship 112-3
Central Co-operative Bank 70
Central Puppet Theatre 80
Centre for Bulgarian Studies
vii, 4, 13
ceramics 160
chairlifts 166-7
Chalcolithic Age 62, 65
Chaprašikova, E. 70
Cherni Vruh 171
Cherniya Kos 185
child care 17
Chilingirov, S. 125

Chinese Embassy 101
Cholakova, M. 80-2
Christoff, B. 144
Church Slavonic 177
churches 27-32, 38-45, 98-9,
114-6, 120-3, 169-71.
*See also under the name
of individual churches,
e.g.* Sedmochislenitsi,
Sveti
cinema 111-3
City Art Gallery 96
City of Sofia, Museum of the
vii, 14, 16, 44, 67
City of Truth 151-3
civic committees 18-23
climate 181
clothes 135, 157
coffee 17, 49, 138
cognac 188
coins 44-5, 159
Commodus 26
Communism 10, 18-22, 26,
36, 42, 60, 88-90, 101,
116, 125, 128, 151-8, 176
compensation 131
condoms 138
Conservative Party 91
Constantine the Great 27
Constantinople 32, 38
Copper Age 62, 65
covered market 27
crafts 96-8, 158
Crampton, R. 195
currency 188-9
customs 188-9

210

OLEANDER TRAVEL BOOKS

THE AEOLIAN ISLANDS
Philip Ward

ALBANIA: A TRAVEL GUIDE
Philip Ward

BAHRAIN: A TRAVEL GUIDE
Philip Ward

BANGKOK: PORTRAIT OF A CITY
Philip Ward

BULGARIA: A TRAVEL GUIDE
Philip Ward

BULGARIAN VOICES: LETTING THE PEOPLE SPEAK
Philip Ward

COME WITH ME TO IRELAND
Philip Ward

FINNISH CITIES: Travels in Helsinki, Turku,
Tampere and Finnish Lapland
Philip Ward

INDIAN MANSIONS: A Social History of the Haveli
Sarah Tillotson

JAPANESE CAPITALS: A Cultural, Historical and
Artistic Guide to Nara, Kyoto and Tokyo
Philip Ward

POLISH CITIES: Travels in Cracow and the South,
Gdañsk, Malbork and Warsaw
Philip Ward

RAJASTHAN, AGRA, DELHI: A Travel Guide
Philip Ward

ROSSYA: A RAIL JOURNEY THROUGH SIBERIA
Michael Pennington

SOFIA: PORTRAIT OF A CITY
Philip Ward

SOUTH INDIA: Tamil Nadu, Kerala, Goa
Philip Ward

SUDAN TALES: Wives in the Sudan Political Service
Rosemary Kenrick

WESTERN INDIA: Bombay, Maharashtra, Karnataka
Philip Ward

WIGHT MAGIC: Tales of the Isle of Wight
Philip Ward

ARABIA PAST AND PRESENT

THE OLEANDER PRESS

BEFRIENDING: A Sociological Case-History
M. Hagard and V. Blickem

BIOGRAPHICAL MEMOIRS OF EXTRAORDINARY PAINTERS
William Beckford

CELTIC: A Comparative Study
D.B. Gregor

A DICTIONARY OF COMMON FALLACIES. 2 vols.
Philip Ward

THE EMPEROR'S GUEST: The Diary of a British PoW of the
Japanese in Indonesia
D.R. Peacock

FATHER GANDER'S NURSERY RHYMES
Per Gander

FORGOTTEN GAMES: A Novel of Cortés and Moctezuma
Philip Ward

FRENCH KEY WORDS
Xavier-Yves Escande

FRIULAN: Language and Literature
D.B. Gregor

FROM THE LION ROCK: Radio Plays
Carey Harrison

THE GERMAN LEFT SINCE 1945
W.D. Graf

GREGUERIAS
Ramón Gómez de la Serna

ITALIAN KEY WORDS
Gianpaolo Intronati

LIBYAN MAMMALS
Ernst Hufnagl

THE LIFE & MURDER OF HENRY MORSHEAD
Ian Morshead

A LIFETIME'S READING
Philip Ward

ROMAGNOL: Language and Literature
D.B. Gregor

SPANISH KEY WORDS
Pedro Casal